THE UNTOLD STORY
OF THE
NEW TESTAMENT
CHURCH

An Extraordinary Guide
to Understanding
the New Testament

FRANK VIOLA

Destiny Image₀ Publishers, Inc.
P.O. Box 310
Shippensburg, PA 17257-0310

"Speaking to the Purposes of God
for This Generation and for the Generations to Come"

ISBN 0-7684-2236-1

For Worldwide Distribution
Printed in the U.S.A.

This book and all other Destiny Image, Revival Press, MercyPlace, Fresh Bread, Destiny Image Fiction, and Treasure House books are available at Christian bookstores and distributors worldwide.

4 5 6 7 8 9 10 / 10 09 08 07 06

For a U.S. bookstore nearest you, call **1-800-722-6774**.
For more information on foreign distributors, call **717-532-3040**.
Or reach us on the Internet:
www.destinyimage.com

With deepest love and appreciation,
to an angel who lives on earth,
my mother—Jeanette.

ENDORSEMENTS

Many of us have been challenged by Frank's previous books examining New Testament church life and practice. Now with this story, focused on helping us see the church in its New Testament context, but in appropriate chronological order, we are greatly helped to understand the various letters of the New Testament. When you see the writings of Peter and Paul and John and the context into which they wrote, it helps make the *why* of their letters as clear as the *what*! Read this book at one sitting and you will marvel as the story of the early church unfolds before your very eyes.

Tony Dale, editor
House 2 House magazine

This volume has provided much needed information that is now in one place for the first time! Read it as I did with a highlighter pen in hand! Thanks, Frank, for the way you let the Lord use you in preparing this for the rest of us!

Ralph W. Neighbour, Jr., author
Where Shall We Go From Here?

Frank Viola has produced a useful and engaging account of the New Testament Church, helpfully setting people and events within their first-century cultural context. While not everyone will agree with every detail of the author's reconstruction or theological interpretation, for any such retelling unavoidably involves some interpretation, still this account helps contemporary believers more fully appreciate the remarkable dynamism of our earliest Christian forebears.

Howard A. Snyder, author
The Community of the King
Liberating the Laity
A Kingdom Manifesto
Decoding the Church

Frank Viola has given us a different kind of church history, a history not of the institution but of the Body. It focuses on the people of God and their struggles; on Paul and his converts, enemies, disciples, and friends; on Peter and John and the churches they birthed and raised. Frank's book emphasizes what went forward among the saints to create eternal value rather than what happened politically to create the church of subsequent centuries. Although most history is written by the winners to justify their victory, *The Untold Story* gives us a history of the early churches as God's own people, whether they were ultimately victorious or troubled.

Hal Miller, author
Christian Community: Biblical or Optional?

Frank Viola has done it again! This time he weaves the New Testament together in a single, chronological story. I love it! We will be promoting this book and I will be giving it to friends this year as gifts.

Nate Krupp, author
God's Simple Plan for His Church

CONTENTS

FOREWORD

Frank Viola has done the world a huge favor. He has "straightened out" the NT (New Testament) for us! The Bible we have today is fully inspired, yes. But the *order* of the NT epistles is—well—a complete jumble. Instead of being arranged by date, they are arranged by size!

I have a scholarly friend who owns over a thousand books. He went on vacation once, leaving his home in the care of a brand-new but eager housekeeper. When he returned home, she had lovingly arranged all of his books by size. He was not pleased.

Yet that is exactly what you and I face every time we open our NTs. It is a bit of a Chinese puzzle. In actual fact, Galatians was the first letter that Paul wrote. But someone in the second century threw together today's NT by putting the four Gospels and Acts at the beginning, then arranging Paul's letters by putting his longest letter first (Romans) and his shortest letter last (Philemon). Then he tacked on all the other letters of the NT. That was not an inspired process! And no scholar claims it was.

But even if someone today were to arrange the NT in order, with the earliest books first, you would still have a lifetime chore on your hands. You would still have to figure out *why* each book was written…just *who* all those strange-named people were who the NT authors wrote to…and *how* those letters were used to accomplish God's eternal purpose all over the Roman Empire! In short, you would still not be able to see the magnificent forest of the early church for all the trees (the blizzard of names, cities, voyages, and letters). But all these things will come alive for you as Frank unfolds the NT story year after year.

Even more important, you will for the first time see and feel the epic drama of the Eternal God unfolding His master plan for the ages. Before your very eyes, the chaotic swirl of first-century people and events will fall into place, and you will be greatly encouraged. Why? Because the drama is not yet over, friend. Today, you and I are once again being called to complete what our brothers and sisters began in Century One: to show forth and express Jesus Christ in open, saving, healing communities that are building the Kingdom of God.

It is our high privilege today to complete the victory in the battle they began. The drama goes on, with the initiative in your hands and mine.

Yet we cannot truly appreciate the immensity of the work we are engaged in unless we pick up the story line at its start. So let us go back with Frank to the earliest beginnings, in the time before time, when the Lamb was slain before the foundation of the world.

James H. Rutz, author
The New Christianity
Colorado Springs, Colorado

One can always read some kind of meaning into a verse of Scripture. But those who understand that the books of the New Testament were written to specific people, in specific places, nearly two thousand years ago, know that this is not a good idea. If the New Testament texts were written to make sense to people in the first century, then we must try to put ourselves into their places in order to determine what the writers of the New Testament intended their readers to understand by what they wrote. If we try to make sense of the Bible with no knowledge of the people who wrote it, those who read it and the society in which they lived, we will be inclined to read into the Scriptures our own society's values and ideas. This would be a major mistake since our culture is very different from that of the ancient Romans.[1]

1.   James Jeffers, *The Greco-Roman World of the New Testament Era: Exploring the Background of Early Christianity* (Downers Grove: InterVarsity Press, 1999), p. 11.

PREFACE

The following pages present the unfolding drama of the NT church in chronological order. A large portion of this drama is based on the narrative of Luke. Luke authored a two-volume work known as *Luke-Acts*. The first volume, the Gospel of Luke, narrates the story of Jesus in the days of His flesh from Galilee to Jerusalem. The second volume, the Acts of the Apostles, narrates the story of Jesus—now in the Spirit working through His Body—from Jerusalem to Rome.[2]

The Untold Story of the New Testament Church is unique in that it blends together the drama we find in Acts with the rest of the NT, thus producing one fluid story. It also guides readers through each NT letter in chronological order, giving them the historical background behind every one of them. In this way, this book is a cross between a narrative commentary and a Bible handbook.

One would think that the story of the first-century Christians is commonly known by those who read and study their Bibles. But it is not. More startling, the vast majority of pastors, Bible teachers, and seminary professors are woefully ignorant of it. The reason for this has to do with how modern ministers are trained today. That bears explaining.

In the typical seminary or Bible college, there is a fundamental disconnect between church history and the NT letters. The seminary student studies the events mentioned in the Book of Acts in a "church history"

---

2.   Both the Gospel of Luke and Acts cover about a 32-year period of time. (Luke covers 4 B.C. to A.D. 30; Acts covers A.D. 30 to A.D. 62.) Further, both volumes are about the same length. Ancient historiographers in the Greek tradition tried to keep the volumes of a historical series they were writing the same size and proportion. Interestingly, the last 23 percent of Luke's Gospel chronicles the events leading to Jesus' trial and death. The last 24 percent of Acts chronicles the events leading to Paul's trial and imprisonment.

course. He then learns to exegete (interpret and expound) the letters of the NT in a "NT studies" class. The result: What God has joined together man has put asunder.[3] A free-flowing story that harmonizes the narrative of Acts with the NT letters is woefully lacking in the curriculum.

A valuable skill that seminary affords is the ability to exegete Scripture. In this way, seminary students become masters at analyzing the individual Books of the Bible. They are like ecologists who analyze the composition of a tree. They are trained to uncover the bark, examine the sap, place the roots under a microscope, and dissect the leaves. But they miss the drama for the details and are blinded from seeing the larger shape of the forest.

Once they step back and survey the entire forest, they are then able to see how each tree came into being, at what point in the forest it was planted, and its relationship to the other trees. Learning the story of the NT church affords one with this broader perspective.[4]

As you read through the following pages, keep in mind that scholars dispute the date and origin of some of our NT books. In this regard, I have largely followed the conclusions of F.F. Bruce, Donald Guthrie, and John A.T. Robinson. As for the chronological sequence and dating of each NT event, I have mostly followed the chronology found in the *Berkeley Version of the New Testament*.

The book is divided up into five sections. Each section represents a specific "motion" that God has taken to fulfill His eternal purpose. The five sections are as follows:

- The First Motion: God's eternal plan is conceived in eternity past.
- The Second Motion: God sends His Son to the earth to lay the groundwork for His eternal plan. Jesus and the Twelve prefigure God's eternal plan in Galilee.
- The Third Motion: The church is born, and God's eternal plan finds visible expression on the earth. Chapters 6-8

---

3. The Book of Acts and the Epistles are part of the same NT canon. Therefore, the information that is contained in the Epistles should be used to fill in the blanks that appear in the story of Acts, and the story of Acts should be used to shed light on the Epistles. This book attempts to do both.

4. For a discussion on the practical implications of the story (which are staggering), see my series on radical church reform: *Rethinking the Wineskin (Vol. 1)*; *Who is Your Covering? (Vol. 2)*; *Pagan Christianity (Vol. 3)*; *So You Want to Start a House Church? (Vol. 4)*; *From Nazareth to Patmos: The Saga of the New Testament Church (Vol. 5)*.

are largely a re-telling of Acts 1-12. The book hits its stride in Chapter 9 where it begins to unfold the background of every NT Epistle.

- The Fourth Motion: God sends His Son back to earth to consummate His eternal plan.
- The Final Motion: God's eternal plan resumes in eternity future.

The sources that I have used in compiling the story appear in a bibliography at the end of the book. I have also chosen to limit the amount of sociological and historical detail lest my readers get distracted from the free-flowing story. Those wishing to obtain further details or verify my conclusions should consult the bibliography. Endnotes appear after each chapter. The endnotes provide important Biblical and historical references that both expand and support my conclusions. Vital information about each NT letter, Paul's apostolic journeys, and the sociological conditions of the first-century appear in gray boxes. You will want to read all the boxes as they are an important part of the story.

Also note that when you read the word "church" in this volume, do not think of a denomination, a building, or a religious service. The word "church" in the NT is translated from the Greek word *ekklesia*, and it means an assembly—or gathering—of the members of a community. To put it another way, the church is the *community* of those who believe on Jesus Christ and who *gather* together to express Him. This is the original meaning of the word, and it is the one that will be used throughout this book.

Finally, I would like to acknowledge my indebtedness to Gene Edwards for inspiring and challenging me to create a holistic model of the early church. His pioneering research and keen insight into this all-too neglected field has laid a solid foundation for me and others to build upon.[5] I am also indebted to F.F. Bruce, Donald Guthrie, and Ben Witherington for their superb scholarship and careful analysis of early church history. Special thanks also goes to Frank Valdez and Mike Biggerstaff for proofing the manuscript, and to Curt Shirley for creating the map illustrations.

My hope in penning this volume is that the Lord would use it to give His people a new and impacting glimpse of early church history…which is really *His story*.

Frank Viola
Jacksonville, Florida

---

5.   Edwards has written a series of books called *First-Century Diaries* (SeedSowers) that tells the story of the first-century church in novel form. His series is aimed at the right brain while the book you hold in your hands is aimed at the left brain.

The arrangement of the letters of Paul in the New Testament is in general that of their length. When we rearrange them into their chronological order, fitting them as far as possible into their life-setting within the record of the Acts of the Apostles, they begin to yield up more of their treasure; they become self-explanatory, to a greater extent than when this background is ignored.[6]

---

6.   G.C.D. Howley in "The Letters of Paul," *New International Bible Commentary* (Grand Rapids: Zondervan, 1979), p. 1095.

INTRODUCTION

Have you ever read your Bible without understanding what you were reading? Have you ever read any of Paul's letters and wondered, *What did he mean when he penned this verse? Whom was this letter written to specifically? What were the people like to whom he wrote? Where was Paul when he wrote, and what was he feeling? What events prompted Paul to write this letter in the first place?*

Have you ever read through the Book of Acts and thought to yourself, *When exactly did these events take place? And at what point in this riveting epic did Paul, Peter, James, John, and Jude pen their letters? How do all of the Books in the NT fit together? What special historical events were occurring during the first century, and what influence did they have on the early church?*

This book answers these questions and more. What is contained in these pages is a chronological-sociological-historical synopsis of the entire NT. Its purpose is to provide you with a panoramic view of the first-century church in its chronological and socio-historical setting. The value of having such a view is priceless.

First, understanding the story of the NT church will give you a whole new understanding of each NT letter—an understanding that is rich, accurate, and exciting. You will be ushered into the living, breathing atmosphere of the first century. You will taste what went on in the writers' hearts when they penned their letters. The circumstances they addressed will be made plain. The people to whom they wrote will come to life.

No longer will you see the Epistles as sterile, complicated reads. Instead, they will turn into living, breathing voices that are part of a living, breathing story. The result? You will grasp the NT like never before! NT scholar F.F. Bruce once made the statement that reading the letters of Paul is like hearing one side of a telephone conversation. This book reconstructs "the other side."

Second, understanding the story will help you see "the big picture" that undergirds the events that followed the birth of the church and its subsequent growth. This "big picture" has at its center an unbroken pattern of God's working. And this pattern reflects God's ultimate goal—which is to have a community on this earth that expresses His nature in a visible way. This theme of a God-ordained community constitutes a unifying thread that runs throughout the entire Bible from Genesis to Revelation. Therefore, reading this book will not only help you to better understand your NT, it will also give you a fresh look at God's eternal purpose...that which is closest to His heart.

Third, understanding the story of the NT church will supply you with the proper historical context which will enable you to *accurately* apply Scripture to your own life. Christians routinely take verses out of context and misapply them to their daily living. Seeing the Scripture in its proper historical context will safeguard you from making this all-too common mistake.

Fourth, understanding the story will forever deliver you from the "cut-and-paste" approach to Bible study that dominates evangelical thinking today. What is the "cut-and-paste" approach to Bible study? It is the common practice of coming to the NT with scissors and glue, clipping and then pasting disjointed sentences (verses) together from Books that were written decades apart.

This "cut-and-paste" approach has spawned all sorts of spiritual hazards—one of them being the popular practice of lashing verses together to build floatable doctrines. Another is that of "proof-texting" to win theological arguments. (A vast majority of Western Christianity behaves as if the mere citation of some random and de-contexualized verse ends all discussion on virtually all subjects.)

The Medievals called this "cut-and-paste" method "a string-of-pearls." You take one text, find some remote metaphorical connection with another text, and voilá, an ironclad doctrine is born! But this is a pathetic approach to understanding the Bible. While it is great for reading one's own biases into the text, it is horrible for understanding the intent of the biblical authors.

It has been rightly said that a person can prove *anything* by taking Bible verses out of context. Let me demonstrate how one can "biblically" prove that it is God's will for believers to commit suicide. All you have to do is lift two verses out of their historical setting and paste them together:

"And he [Judas]...*went...and hanged himself"* (Matthew 27:5).
"Then said Jesus... 'Go and do the same' " (Luke 10:37b).

While this is an outrageous example of the "cut-and-paste" approach, it makes a profound point. Without understanding the historical context of the NT, Christians have managed to build doctrines and invent practices that have fragmented the Body of Christ into thousands of denominations. Understanding the sequence of each NT Book and the socio-historical setting that undergirds them is one remedy for this problem.[7]

I have stated four reasons why rediscovering the NT story is a worthwhile endeavor. But there is one more reason. There is a very good chance that it will revolutionize your Christian life and your relationship with your Lord.

---

7. The Books that make up our NT are grossly out of sequence. When the NT canon was compiled during the second century, Paul's epistles were arranged according to their length rather than according to their dates. Chapter divisions were added in the year 1227 and verse divisions were inserted in 1551. See my book, *Pagan Christianity*, Chapter 11 for a detailed account of how this happened and its effects.

We make the basic assumption that an author was trying to communicate something meaningful to the audience for which he or she wrote. This approach attempts to discover who wrote the text, when it was written, and what issues it was intended to address in its own time. Only when we grasp the historical situation of both author and audience can we hope to understand the message communicated.[8]

---

8.   David L. Barr, *An Introduction: New Testament Story* (New York: Wadsworth Publishing Company, 1995), p. 6.

PROLOGUE

We are now ready to begin our journey. Find a comfortable place to sit. Grab your favorite version of the NT, and lay it by your side. I now introduce you to the most remarkable story in the world...the untold story of the first-century church.

The story begins in the dateless past...

CHAPTER 1

THE FIRST MOTION:
THE GODHEAD IN ETERNITY PAST

May they all be one, just as You, Father, are in Me and I am in You. May they also be one in Us, so that the world may believe You sent Me. I have given them the glory that You have given to Me. May they be one just as We are one. I am in them and You are in Me. May they be made completely one, so that the world may know You sent Me and that You have loved them just as You have loved Me (John 17:21-23).

And to shed light for all about the administration of the mystery hidden for ages in God who created all things. This is so that God's multi-faceted wisdom may now be made known through the church to the rulers and authorities in the heavens. This is according to the purpose of the ages, which He made in the Messiah, Jesus our Lord (Ephesians 3:9-11).

...The hope of eternal life that God, who cannot lie, promised before time began (Titus 1:2).

It is a time before time. Nothing exists except the Trinitarian Community: God the Father, God the Son, and God the Holy Spirit. God is *All.*

Among the three Persons of the Godhead,[1] there is unbroken fellowship between the Father and the Son by means of the Spirit. A council is held. God conceives a plan. He shrouds this plan in a mystery, and He hides it in the Son. The plan will be disclosed at an appointed time far into the future. Paul of Tarsus will later call this timeless plan "the purpose of the ages"[2] and "the mystery."[3]

What is this plan? It is this: In eternity past, the Godhead purposes to one day expand its fellowship to a people not yet created. Put another way, God wills to produce a community on earth that will reflect the community that is found among the Father, the Son, and the Spirit.

God, who sees the end from the beginning, takes the first step in carrying out this plan. Within the Eternal Son are hidden ones whom God has chosen to be part of His ordained community.[4] The names of the hidden ones are written in an eternal volume called "the Book of Life."[5]

Within the Godhead there is a Lamb. This Lamb is God the Son. At a future date God will symbolize this Lamb by a created animal called by the same name. This Lamb exists now...in eternity past...and He is slain.[6] God completes all things before He creates all things.[7]

God's "eternal purpose" provokes Him to create a universe and an earth. He weaves into His creation pictures and symbols of His Son and of this future community that will express His nature. God then chooses a people for Himself: The nation of Israel. Israel's entire life and history prefigures the spiritual community that will one day display God's eternal nature on the earth.[8]

ENDNOTES

1. The "Godhead" is the biblical and theological term for what is commonly known as the "Trinity"—the Father, Son, and Holy Spirit. See Acts 17:29; Romans 1:20; Colossians 2:9 (KJV).

2. Ephesians 1:11; 3:11; 2 Timothy 1:9.

3. Romans 16:25; Ephesians 1:9; 3:3-9; Colossians 1:26; 2:2.

4. Ephesians 1:4.

5. Revelation 17:8; 20:12; 21:27.

6. 1 Peter 1:19-20; Revelation 13:8.

7. Hebrews 4:3.

8. Acts 7:38; Romans 2:28-29; 1 Corinthians 10:1ff; Galatians 6:16; Colossians 2:16ff.; Hebrews 10:1ff.

Chapter 2

The Second Motion: The Son Is Sent to Earth

But when the completion of the time came, God sent His Son, born of a woman, born under the law (Galatians 4:4).

The appointed time has come. God the Father sends the Eternal Son into the earth. The Son will become the embodiment of all the symbols embedded in creation. He will also fulfill all that the nation of Israel foreshadowed.[1]

The Son will come into the earth to manifest and embody God's eternal purpose for mankind. He will also die for the sins of the world and be raised again as the Head of a new race—a race that was chosen before the foundation of the world—a race that will include both Jew and Gentile.[2] The Son will come into the world to establish the community that the Godhead purposed in the timeless past.[3]

ENDNOTES

1. Hosea 11:1; Matt. 2:15; Col. 2:16–17; Heb. 6–10.

2. Col. 1–2; Eph. 1–3; 1 Cor. 10:32. The second-Century Christians referred to themselves as "the third Race."

3. Matt. 16:18; Eph. 5:25-27.

CHAPTER 3

THE NAZARETH CHRONICLE

4 B.C.–A.D. 28

... "She will give birth to a son, and you are to name Him Jesus, because He will save His people from their sins." Now all this took place to fulfill what was spoken by the Lord through the prophet: See, the virgin will be with child and give birth to a son, and they will name Him Immanuel, which is translated "God is with us" (Matthew 1:21-23).

Divinity takes on humanity. The Son of God penetrates the womb of Mary and is born in Bethlehem. He is raised in the ill-reputed town of Nazareth and comes to be known as "Jesus of Nazareth." In Nazareth, Jesus experiences fellowship with His Father just as He knew it in eternity past. Jesus is a carpenter by trade. He lives thirty years on earth before He begins His earthly ministry.[1]

The Trinitarian Community is present in our Lord's rib cage as He communes with His Father through the indwelling Spirit. The Community of the Father, Son, and Spirit dwells inside of Him.[2] The eternal fellowship that exists within the Godhead continues unbroken. It simply moves from the heavens to the earth where Jesus has taken up residence.

ENDNOTES

1. Matt. 1–3; Mark 6; Luke 1–4.
2. Col. 2:9.

CHAPTER 4

THE GALILEAN CHRONICLE

A.D. 28–A.D. 30

Then He went up the mountain and summoned those He wanted, and they came to Him. He appointed Twelve, whom He also named apostles, that they might be with Him and that He might send them out to preach (Mark 3:13-14).

In Galilee, Jesus calls twelve men to live with Him for three years.[1] He trains these men to take His place after He leaves the earth. The twelve men are:[2]

- Andrew (brother of Peter)
- Bartholomew (also called Nathanael)
- James, son of Zebedee
- James, son of Alphaeus
- John, son of Zebedee
- Judas Iscariot
- Judas (also called Lebbaeus and surnamed Thaddaeus)
- Matthew (also called Levi)
- Peter (also called Simon and Cephas)
- Philip
- Simon the Zealot[3] (also called Simon the Canaanite)
- Thomas (also called Didymus)

For three years, the Lord Jesus brings the Twelve into the same experience that He knew in Nazareth.[4] That is, just as the Son fellowships with His Father, the Twelve learn to fellowship with the Son.

Jesus also brings the Twelve into a foreshadowing experience of the community that God wishes to have on the earth. The Twelve will become the primitive embryo of this community. They have informal, simple gatherings around Jesus where He is central and the object of worship and fellowship.

ENDNOTES

1. Mark 3:13ff.
2. Matthew 10:2-4, Mark 3:14-19, Luke 6:13-16.
3. The Zealots were a Jewish revolutionary group violently opposed to Roman rule over Palestine. This militant wing of the Jewish independence movement took the lead in the revolt against Rome in A.D. 66.
4. Luke 6–23.

Chapter 5

The Hingepin of the Drama: Calvary

A.D. 30

For I passed on to you as most important what I also received: that Christ died for our sins according to the Scriptures, that He was buried, that He was raised on the third day according to the Scriptures, and that He appeared to Cephas, then to the Twelve. Then He appeared to over 500 brothers at one time, most of whom remain to the present, but some have fallen asleep (1 Corinthians 15:3-6).

Spring, A.D. 30

It is four days before Passover.[1] Every Israelite family has secured a spotless lamb. The lambs are set aside for four days of preparation. On this same day, Jesus, the Christ (Messiah), enters the city of Jerusalem.[2]

Friday, April 7, 30[3]

From noon to 3:00 p.m. the cries of the spotless lambs fill Jerusalem as they are slaughtered for the Passover feast. At the same time, Jesus Christ—the *real* Lamb of God—is crucified.[4] As Jesus breathes His last breath, an earthquake hits the land, and the curtain (veil) which encloses the Most Holy Place in the temple is rent in two, from top to bottom.[5] This signifies that the way to fellowship with the Father has now been opened for all men to experience.[6]

Through His death, Jesus solves the entire problem of man's fall and satan's rebellion.[7] Joseph of Arimathea, a wealthy member of the Sanhedrin and a disciple of Jesus, places Christ's body in a new and unused tomb.[8]

Sunday, April 9, 30

The feast of the sheaf of firstfruits has arrived. An Israelite walks into a field and locates the first sheaf of barley that has sprung up. The blade demonstrates that there will be a coming harvest. The Israelite pulls the sprig out of the ground and hands it to a priest. The priest waves the barley sheaf in the temple before Jehovah. At the same moment, the Lord Jesus Christ comes out of the tomb as the Firstfruits of all who will rise from the dead.[9]

Jesus was put into the earth as a corn of wheat, suffering death alone. But on this morning, He has resurrected as a new grain which has sprouted—with many others to follow.[10]

After His resurrection, Jesus meets with the Twelve and breathes the Holy Spirit into them.[11] Jesus Christ now indwells the Twelve, just as His Father indwelt Him.

Christ stays on the earth for 40 days, during which time He intermittently appears to the Twelve. He also appears to 500 of His followers. When He appears, He speaks to them about the Kingdom of God.[12]

After the 40 days are complete, Jesus meets with the Twelve on the Mount of Olives. He sends them out to preach the gospel and found the church.[13] But they are commanded to wait in Jerusalem until their sending is activated. They are told to wait for the promise of the Spirit.[14]

May 19, 30

Jesus Christ disappears in a cloud and ascends into the heavens where He takes His seat at the right hand of His Father.[15] Jesus Christ enters His present-day ministry of High Priest for His people.[16] As the Twelve strain their eyes to see Him vanish, two white-robed men stand before them and assure them that Jesus will return in the same way that He ascended.

The Twelve walk a Sabbath day's journey (three quarters of a mile) from the Mount of Olives to the city of Jerusalem. They are accompanied by 108 other disciples (followers) of Jesus.[17]

Jesus Christ is now the crucified, risen, ascended, enthroned Lord of glory! His work on Calvary has paved the way for His church—the community that will express His nature—to be built on the earth.

ENDNOTES

1. The Passover feast is described in Exodus 12–13.

2. Matthew 21:1ff; Mark 11:1ff; John 12:1ff.

3. April 7, A.D. 30 is the traditional date for the Lord's death. Some contemporary scholars prefer April 3, 33 as the more accurate date. And some believe that Christ was crucified on a Wednesday or Thursday. See Harold Hoenher's classic work, *Chronological Aspects of the Life of Christ* (Zondervan).

4. Matthew 26:2; John 19–21; 1 Corinthians 5:7; 1 Peter 1:19; Hebrews 9:14.

5. Matthew 27:50-51; Mark 15:37-38.

6. Hebrews 10:19-20. Historically, God dwelt on top of the ark of the covenant in the Most Holy Place of the temple where He would fellowship with man (see Exodus 25:22ff; Hebrews 9:1-8). Up until this point, the only person who was allowed to penetrate the curtain (veil) that enclosed the Most Holy Place was the high priest. And he could only enter it once a year. When Jesus died, He made a way for all of God's people to enter the Holy of Holies (spiritually speaking) and fellowship with God.

7. Romans 5–7; Galatians 6:14; Colossians 1:20; 2:14-15; Ephesians 2:14-16; Hebrews 2:14-15.

8. Matthew 27:57-60; Mark 15:42-26; Luke 23:50-53; John 19:41-42.

9. Leviticus 23:10ff; 1 Corinthians 15:23.

10. John 12:23-24.

11. John 20:21-22.

12. Acts 1:3; 1 Corinthians 15:4-7.

13. The word *apostle* means "sent one." Apostles, or apostolic workers, are people who are called by God to plant churches, i.e, they are "church planters." (See my book *So You Want to Start a House Church?* for details.)

14. Luke 24:49; Acts 1:1-12.

15. Romans 8:34; Ephesians 1:20; Colossians 3:1; Hebrews 1:3; 8:1; 10:12; 12:2; 1 Peter 3:22.

16. Hebrews 2:17–10:21.

17. Acts 1:9-15.

CHAPTER 6

THE THIRD MOTION: THE CHURCH IS BORN

That life was revealed, and we have seen it and we testify and declare to you the eternal life that was with the Father and was revealed to us—what we have seen and heard we also declare to you, so that you may have fellowship along with us; and indeed our fellowship is with the Father and with His Son Jesus Christ (1 John 1:2-3).

In Him we were also made His inheritance, predestined according to the purpose of the One who works out everything in agreement with the decision of His will (Ephesians 1:11).

...And to bring to light what is the administration of the mystery which for ages has been hidden in God, who created all things; in order that the manifold wisdom of God might now be made known through the church to the rulers and authorities in the heavenly places. This was in accordance with the eternal purpose which He carried out in Christ Jesus our Lord...(Ephesians 3:9-11).

[He] has saved us and called us with a holy calling, not according to our works, but according to His own purpose and grace, which was given to us in Christ Jesus before time began (2 Timothy 1:9).

T he following pages contain the story of the early church. The church—the *ekklesia*—is the community that God has had in view since the dateless past—a community that will express His Divine nature in the earth. The church is made up of the hidden ones who were chosen and hid in the Son before time began. When the church is born, the hidden ones will begin to be manifested. God's eternal purpose of expanding the Divine fellowship that exists within the Godhead finds its fulfillment in and through the church.[1]

ENDNOTE

1. Ephesians 3:9-11.

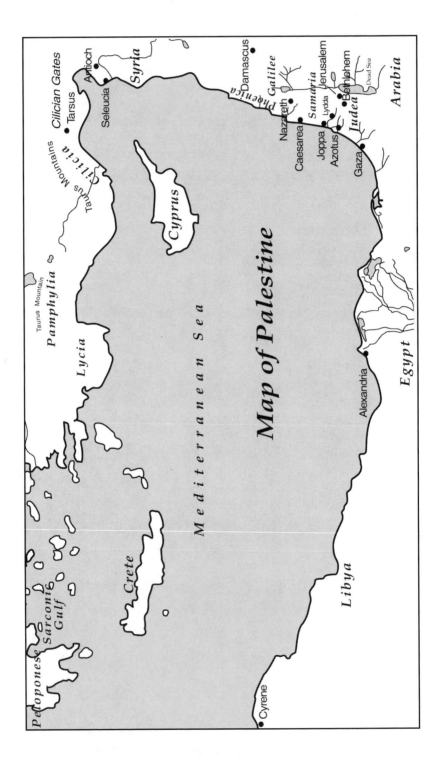

CHAPTER 7

THE JERUSALEM CHRONICLE
A.D. 30–A.D. 41

So those who accepted his message were baptized, and that day about 3,000 people were added to them. And they devoted themselves to the apostles' teaching, to fellowship, to the breaking of bread, and to prayers (Acts 2:41-42).

Approximately 120 Jewish disciples of Jesus hold a prayer meeting in the upper room of a house in Jerusalem where they all have been living. The house probably belongs to Mary, John Mark's mother.[1] The Twelve are present.[2] Also in attendance are Mary, the mother of Jesus, the brothers of Jesus (James, Jude, Joseph, and Simon),[3] and some women.

Peter speaks to the group and convinces them from a prophecy in the Psalms that someone must replace Judas Iscariot. (Judas committed suicide after he betrayed Jesus.) Joseph (also known as Barsabbas and Justus) and Matthias are nominated to replace Judas.[4] Both men have been with Jesus from the beginning of His ministry. The Twelve pray for God to select the right man. They cast lots,[5] and the lot falls to Matthias, who is added to the Twelve.[6]

Sunday, May 29, 30

It is the day of Pentecost. Hebrew-speaking Jews, Greek-speaking Jews, and proselytes (Gentiles by birth who converted to Judaism) from all across the Roman Empire have swelled the city of Jerusalem to celebrate the feast. Among the nations represented are: Parthians, Medes, Elamites, residents of Mesopotamia, Judea, Cappadocia, Pontus, Asia Minor, Phrygia, Pamphylia, Egypt, Lybia, Rome, Crete, and Arabia.

> *Sharpening the Focus:* The Roman Empire is presently enjoying the *Pax Romana* ("Roman peace") which Emperor Augustus (ruled 27 B.C. to A.D. 14) established from Spain to the Black Sea, from Egypt to the English Channel. For the most part, life in the empire is secure and trade is safe. There are between 70 and 100 million

people living in the Roman Empire. One half are slaves. (The Empire is run on slave labor. Slaves have no legal rights and are viewed as the personal property of their masters. Some wealthy Romans own as many as 20,000 slaves.) Few in the Roman Empire are part of the wealthy senatorial class. Most belong to the poor plebeian class. More than half the population is dependent on the regular distribution of free grain. Ninety percent of the Empire's workers are in farming and herding.

There are between three and eight million Jews in the Empire. Two thirds of them live outside of Palestine. These are called the Dispersion (*Diaspora*). Because the Jews have strange beliefs (they serve only one God) and strange practices (keeping the Sabbath and not eating pork), they are despised by most Greeks and Romans. (Many Greeks and Romans view circumcision as mutilation, the Sabbath as a cloak for laziness, and Jewish dietary laws as foolishness.) Yet Judaism is tolerated and protected under Roman law.

Jerusalem is a city that is less than one square mile. The normal population is estimated at 60,000. Most are Jewish. During the Pentecost celebration, there is an estimated 125,000-500,000 added to the population. Luke mentions sixteen different countries that are represented to celebrate the feast. The city is composed of the very rich, the destitute, as well as craftsmen and merchants. First-century Jerusalem is the most distinguished city in the east.

The NT uses the phrase "going up" when describing those traveling to Jerusalem. The city is 2,300 feet above sea level. Most residents speak and only understand Aramaic (Mishnaic Hebrew). Ten to twenty percent of the population speak Greek. Some are bilingual, speaking Greek as their second language. Some speak only Greek. The educated and merchants learn Greek for business purposes. The Romans have a presence in Jerusalem in the Antonia fortress. But they mostly keep to themselves and do not mingle with the populace.

It is 9:00 a.m. A priest has prepared two loaves of leavened bread. He pours oil on them and slips them into an oven to be baked together.[7] At the same moment, the Holy Spirit descends into the upper room where the 120 are staying. The Spirit enters the room with the noise of a rushing mighty windstorm. The Spirit fills the 120 with His presence and power.[8] Tongues of fire appear on their heads, and they speak in languages that they have never learned.[9] As a result, those visiting Jerusalem from around the Roman Empire hear God being magnified in their own language and dialect!

(Significantly, the day of Pentecost has been invested with the commemoration of the giving of the Law. According to Jewish tradition, the Law was supernaturally uttered from Sinai in the 70 languages of the nations of the world.)

The Jerusalem Church Is Born

With the Spirit's coming, Jesus Christ—the *Head*—baptizes 120 Jews into His *Body*. The first church is born on the earth! There is now a community of people who contain God's life and are expressing God's nature! Jesus Christ is being expressed in Jerusalem!

(Spiritually speaking, one of the loaves has been baked. Ten years will pass, and the Lord will baptize Gentiles into this same Body. And the *two* oil-covered loaves that were slipped into an oven on the day of Pentecost will find its fulfillment. The Jew and the Gentile will be baptized into one Body, comprising a new race and new spiritual community.)[10]

The noise from the upper room provokes a crowd of Jews to see what has happened. The Jews are bewildered to hear many of their own dialects from the various nations being spoken by 120 Jerusalem residents. Some question what this strange phenomenon means. Others accuse the 120 of being drunk.

Peter, surrounded by the eleven apostles, stands in the midst of a crowded Jerusalem. He preaches Jesus Christ to a Jewish audience, and exhorts them to repent and be baptized in the name of Jesus. Three thousand Jews respond and are added to the newly formed church. The fellowship of the Trinitarian Community has now broadened from 12 to 120 to 3,000.[11]

The first instinct of these new Christians is to meet and to meet constantly. The Galilean experience of informal gatherings with Christ as center is now brought to Jerusalem by the Twelve. And it is being reproduced among 3,000 people.[12] Those in the church devote themselves to the teaching of the apostles, the Lord's Supper, prayer, and fellowship. The Twelve are performing signs and wonders in the city. The church is in awe as it beholds God's power made visible.

Many of the Jews who have come to Jerusalem for the Pentecostal feast choose to remain in the city. They wish to learn from the twelve apostles rather than to return to their homes. (Jerusalem has the only church on earth!) These piligrims leave their homes, their jobs, and settle in the city. The Jerusalem believers sell their possessions and pool their resources together to take care of their new visitors.

The Jerusalem church is a microcosm of the city. It includes both wealthy and poor as well as a substantial number of Jews who speak Greek only (Hellenists) and Jews who speak Aramaic[13] only or both Aramaic and Greek (Hebrews).

Church Life Begins
A.D. 30-31

Every day, the Twelve minister to the multitudes in Solomon's porch (also called Solomon's colonnade or portico).[14] Solomon's porch is a large open area located on the east side of the outer court of the temple. It is simply a large porch with a roof over it.[15] There the church worships the Lord and hears the apostles preach. The church also meets in homes to take the Lord's Supper, to share meals together, to fellowship, and to worship God. New converts are made daily and are added to the church. The church finds favor with the people of the city.

It is 3:00 p.m.—the Jewish hour of prayer. Peter and John head to the temple to participate in the prayer service. As they approach the temple, they meet a crippled man who has been lame since birth. The man begs beside the temple gate—called "the Beautiful Gate"—every day. ("The Beautiful Gate" is the Nicanor Gate that is made of remarkable Corinthian bronze.)

As Peter and John are about to enter the temple, the man asks them for money. Peter and John do not give him money, for they have none. Instead, they heal the man in the name of Jesus. Fully astounded, the man jumps up on his feet and begins leaping and praising God. He then enters the temple with Peter and John.

Those who see the man walking are shocked and in awe. So they rush into Solomon's colonnade where the man is standing with Peter and John. Taking advantage of their captive audience, Peter and John preach Jesus Christ to them.[16]

The priests, the temple guard, and some Sadducees[17] hear Peter and John preaching Christ and His resurrection. They are very disturbed by the teaching on the resurrection so they seize the two men. Peter and John are arrested and put in jail for the evening. Many who heard the two apostles preach are converted. The Jerusalem church has rapidly grown to 5,000 men. If we count the women and children, the population is at least 10,000.[18]

The next day, Peter and John are brought before the Sanhedrin to be questioned. The Sanhedrin is the senate and supreme court for the Jewish nation. It is both religious and political. It contains 70 members and one presiding high priest. The high priest is regarded as the voice of God on earth. Most of the Sanhedrin's members are from the Sadducee party. Annas, the ex-high priest, is present. Annas' son-in-law, Caiaphas, is the reigning high priest.[19]

The Sanhedrin demands that Peter and John tell them by what power they performed this miracle. Filled with the Holy Spirit, Peter and John preach Jesus Christ to the Sanhedrin!

The Sanhedrin is amazed at the boldness of Peter and John and take note that they had been with Jesus. Since the healed man is standing in their midst, the Sanhedrin cannot deny the miracle. They send Peter and John out of the council chamber and confer amongst themselves. Knowing that they could not deny the miracle, they decide to forbid Peter and John from healing and teaching in the name of Jesus.

The two apostles are called back into the council chamber and hear the Sanhedrin's decision. Peter and John respond that they must obey God rather than man. They explain that they cannot stop speaking about what they have experienced of Christ.

The council threatens the two men further. But it releases them because it does not know how to punish them without causing a riot. Peter and John immediately report to the Jerusalem church what took place. The church has a prayer meeting. The believers ask for boldness, healing power, and the continuation of miracles. The Holy Spirit descends into the building with power, shaking its very foundations. The church is filled with the Holy Spirit, and the apostles continue to preach Jesus Christ with boldness.

The church in Jerusalem is of one heart and one soul. The believers hold everything in common. The twelve apostles bear witness to Christ's resurrection with great power. No one in the church has a need. From time to time, all who own land and property sell them and bring the money to the Twelve. The Twelve distribute the proceeds to all who have need.

One such man is Joseph, a native from the Island of Cyprus and a Levite. Joseph voluntarily sells his land and brings the money to the apostles.[20] Joseph is an encourager, so the apostles nickname him "Barnabas," which means "son of encouragement."[21]

Persecution Begins
A.D. 31-33

Ananias and his wife Sapphira sell some property and give a portion of the sale money to the church. But they lie to the apostles saying they gave the full amount to the church. God shows Peter their deception. Peter makes known their sin and tells them that they have lied to God and not to man. One after the other, Ananias and Sapphira fall to the ground and die. Great fear grips the church as a result.[22]

Many signs and wonders are performed by the hands of the apostles as the Twelve continue to preach Christ in Solomon's colonnade. (The apostles do not leave the city of Jerusalem. And no one except the apostles is preaching the gospel.) Crowds of sick people in Jerusalem and from the neighboring villages bring their sick and demon-possessed into the streets on beds and mats to be healed by the apostles. All are healed. The mere passing of Peter's shadow brings healing to some. Multitudes, both men and women, are brought to the Lord.

The high priest and his friends (who are Sadducees) react with violent jealousy. The Twelve are arrested and put in jail. But an angel delivers them from jail at night. The angel tells the apostles to go back into the temple court and resume preaching Christ. The Twelve obey and enter the temple court at daybreak where they begin preaching again.

When the Sanhedrin gets word of this, the captain of the temple guard and his temple guards re-arrest the Twelve and bring them before the Sanhedrin. The Twelve are questioned, but they answer that they must obey God and not man.

The Sadducees are furious and want to put the Twelve to death. But Gamaliel, the most significant and influential Pharisaic educator of the day and an expert on religious law, persuades the court to leave the men alone. (Rabbi Gamaliel is the greatest teacher of the day, and he is honored by all. He is also the head of his own school in the tradition of Hillel,[23] and Saul of Tarsus is one of his pupils.)[24]

The apostles are flogged. That is, they are given the "forty lashes minus one."[25] The whip they are beaten with is called a scourge. It is made of thirty-nine leather cords tied into three bands of thirteen cords. The cords are weighted with pieces of bone and metal and attached to a stout wooden handle. The apostles are whipped on the back and chest.

The Sanhedrin commands the Twelve to no longer speak in the name of Jesus. After they are released, the Twelve rejoice that they were counted worthy to suffer for the Lord's name. Fearlessly, the Twelve daily declare Jesus Christ in the temple court and in the homes of the believers.[26]

Crisis in Jerusalem
A.D. 33-34

The church of Jerusalem faces its first internal problem. As the church is quickly increasing in number, the Grecian (Hellenistic) Jews begin complaining against the Hebraic (Hebrew) Jews.[27] Every day, the food is equally distributed among the members of the church. However, the Grecian Jews feel that their widows are being overlooked.

To solve this problem, the Twelve gather the whole church together. They explain that they cannot devote any time to this problem as they have their hands full with ministering the Word. So they instruct the church to choose seven men to oversee the food distribution. The men must be spiritual (full of the Spirit) and practical (full of wisdom). The church is pleased with this idea and selects seven men. They are all Grecian Jews. The men are:

- Stephen, a man full of faith, grace, power, and the Holy Spirit
- Procorus
- Parmenas
- Nicolas from Antioch, a convert to Judaism.[28]
- Timon
- Nicanor
- Philip

The church presents these seven men to the Twelve. The Twelve lay hands on the "seven" with prayer. The Word of God advances and the believing community greatly increases. A large company of Jewish priests are converted and added to the church.[29]

Stephen Is Martyred
A.D. 35-37

Stephen, one of the "seven," begins preaching Christ in the city of Jerusalem. He performs signs that confirm the Word. Stephen frequents one of the 365 synagogues in the city—the synagogue of the Freedmen (also called the synagogue of the Libertines).[30] He debates the Grecian Jews who attend there. (The synagogue of the Freedmen is frequented by Jews from Cyrene, Alexandria, Asia, and Cilicia. Saul of Tarsus attends this synagogue and hears Stephen preach.)

The Grecian Jews try to argue with Stephen, but they cannot stand up to his wisdom or the Spirit by which he speaks. So they secretly persuade some to accuse him falsely. They charge Stephen with blaspheming against the temple and the Law of Moses.

This charge causes a violent stir in the synagogue. Stephen is immediately seized by the elders and the teachers of the Law. He is tried before the Sanhedrin on charges that he is preaching Jesus of Nazareth who promised to destroy the temple. The entire court begins to stare at Stephen. Even though they are hostile toward him, they perceive his face to be that of an angel—aglow as one consciously standing in God's presence.

The high priest asks Stephen if the charges are true. Stephen responds with a lengthy defense wherein he surveys the entire OT (Old Testament) and magnifies Jesus Christ in the process. At the end of his defense, he rebukes the Jews for murdering the Messiah and for disobeying God's Law. The Sanhedrin is furious, so much so that they gnash their teeth at him. Stephen looks up to Heaven and sees Jesus, standing (not sitting) at the right hand of God, waiting to receive Stephen.

When the Jews hear this, they cover their ears, scream at the top of their lungs, and drag Stephen out of the city. In a violent rage, they stone him. (The Sanhedrin is allowed to pronounce and execute the death sentence in only one case—offenses against the sanctity of the temple.[31] For this reason, when Jesus was brought to trial before the same court, an attempt was made to convict Him on charges of speaking against the temple.[32] Had that attempt succeeded, it would not have been necessary to refer Jesus' case to Pilate.)

As Stephen is being stoned he prays, "Lord Jesus, receive my spirit."[33] He falls to his knees and adds, "Do not hold this sin against them."[34] Stephen dies a brutal unjust death, being the first martyr of the church. Godly men bury him and mourn his loss.[35]

The Church Is Transplanted Throughout Palestine

Saul of Tarsus, a young man about 30 years of age and a well-known Pharisee, witnesses Stephen's death. He was guarding the clothes of the executioners, showing full support of the brutal slaying.

Saul acts as a commissioner for the Sanhedrin and begins to ravage the church in Jerusalem. He invades their house church meetings, dragging the men and the women into prison. To escape the persecution, the church in Jerusalem disperses throughout Judea, Samaria, and Galilee. Some flee as far as Damascus, Syria—a city 135 miles north of Jerusalem. The Twelve stay behind in Jerusalem and go into hiding.

The believers who scatter throughout Palestine begin to spread the gospel in their new locales. This is the first time that the gospel is being preached outside of Jerusalem. New churches are transplanted all over Palestine as a result. The community of the redeemed has now transplanted itself from Jerusalem to Judea, Galilee, and Samaria. Jesus Christ is now being expressed in these regions. The Twelve leave Jerusalem and begin traveling to establish these new churches.[36] The brothers of Jesus, Jude included, also begin to travel.[37]

Sharpening the Focus: Named after King Saul of Israel, Saul was born a Hebrew of the tribe of Benjamin. He was born around A.D. 5. in the Cilician city of Tarsus. Tarsus is one of the major centers of Hellenistic culture. It is a university town with a large population.

Tarsus is the principal city of Cilicia with a mixed population. The city has a rich past, witnessing the romantic first meeting of Antony and Cleopatra. It is a prosperous city, renowned for its material products, particularly linen (which comes from the flax that grows in the fertile plain of the city) and *cilicium* (which serves as a protective covering made of goat's hair).

"Saul" is his Jewish name. But he was born a Roman citizen (Acts 22:27ff). And Roman citizens have three names: A forename (*praenomen*), a family name (*nomen gentile*), and an additional name (*cognomen*). "Paul" is his additional Roman name (*cognomen*); we do not know his other two names.

As a young boy, Saul is taken to Jerusalem to receive his Hebrew training. It is there that he grows up. He is well educated, speaking Aramaic, Hebrew, Greek and probably Latin.

Saul was mentored under the greatest teacher of the day, Gamaliel. He was trained to be a fanatical Jew—a Pharisee. And he is far more zealous than his peers (Galatians 1:14; Philippians 3:4-6). Since Saul is a Pharisee, he was doubtlessly married at one time. But after he becomes a Christian, he will be unmarried. All Jewish rabbis work for a living. They must learn a skill. Saul's trade is that of a tentmaker. This means that he repairs tents and makes other leather products. This being so, on his travels, Saul will carry a bag of cutting tools, an awl (a pointed tool for making holes in leather), and a sharpening stone.

Philip the Evangelist

Philip, one of "the seven," travels to Samaria and preaches Christ.[38] Philip's preaching is confirmed by miraculous signs, healings, and the casting out of devils. Philip's ministry of deliverance brings great joy to the city. He baptizes both men and women who respond to his message. Simon Magus, a well-known and highly acclaimed sorcerer from Samaria, is baptized also.

The Twelve in Jerusalem get word that some in Samaria have received the gospel. So they send Peter and John to help establish the church.[39] When they arrive, Peter and John lay hands on the new converts and they are baptized with the Holy Spirit. Simon Magus offers money to the apostles in exchange for the ability to impart the Spirit to others. Peter rebukes Simon and exposes his wicked heart. Simon asks Peter to pray that God will not judge him. Peter and John return to Jerusalem, preaching the gospel in many Samaritan villages on the way.

Philip stays in Samaria. But an angel appears to him and tells him to head south to the desert road that leads from Jerusalem to Gaza. Philip responds. And on his way, he meets an Ethiopian eunuch who is a Gentile worshipper of the God of Israel. The eunuch is the official treasurer for Candace, the queen of Ethiopia.[40] The eunuch is heading back home from Jerusalem, where he had visited to worship at one of the Jewish festivals.

The Spirit tells Philip to approach the chariot where the Ethiopian is reading Isaiah 53 aloud. (All reading is done aloud during this time period.) Philip engages the eunuch in a dialogue and leads him to Christ. He then baptizes the eunuch. As soon as the eunuch comes up out of the water, the Holy Spirit snatches Philip away to Azotus, the old Philistine city of Ashdod some 20 miles up the coast from Gaza. The eunuch returns to Ethiopia with the joy of salvation.[41]

From Azotus, Philip preaches the gospel from town to town until he comes to Caesarea (also called Caesarea Maritima or Caesarea-by-the-Sea). Philip will reside in Caesarea for the next 20 years.[42]

Jesus Christ Appears to Saul
A.D. 37-40[43]

Back in Jerusalem, Saul hunts the Christians down and roots them out from wherever they have dispersed. He threatens to murder all Christians and receives permission from the high priest to look for them in all the synagogues of Damascus, Syria where there is a large Jewish population. Saul is permitted to go to Damascus, arrest the Christians there (both men and women), and bring them back to Jerusalem as prisoners. One of his methods of securing capital punishment on the Christians is to lure them to blaspheme.[44]

It is noon. Saul and several of his companions are on their way to Damascus. Suddenly, the Lord Jesus Christ appears to Saul in a blinding light from Heaven! Saul and his companions all fall to the ground. Jesus speaks to Saul and asks him in the Hebrew language, "Saul, Saul, why are you persecuting Me?" Saul's companions see a light and hear a noise, but they do not understand the voice.[45] Jesus tells Saul to stand up. He then tells Saul that He has called him to bring salvation to the Gentiles.

When Saul picks himself up from the ground, he cannot see. So his companions lead him into Damascus by the hand. Saul is blinded for three days, during which time he neither eats nor drinks.

There is a church in Damascus. A faithful brother in Christ named Ananias belongs to it. Jesus calls Ananias in a vision and instructs him to find Saul in the house of Judas on Straight Street. Knowing who Saul is, Ananias expresses doubt. The Lord reassures Ananias that Saul is a chosen vessel who will bring salvation to the Gentiles, and he will suffer greatly as a result of that calling.

Ananias finds Saul, lays his hands on him, and confirms his calling to go to the Gentiles. Saul receives healing for his temporary blindness and is filled with the Spirit. Ananias then baptizes Saul.

Saul eats and regains his strength. He stays with the church in Damascus for a short time and immediately begins preaching Christ in the synagogues.[46] Those who hear him are astonished, for they know he had previously persecuted the Christians. Saul grows more and more powerful, baffling the Jews and demonstrating from the OT Scriptures that Jesus is the Messiah.

Saul vanishes to Arabia for about three years,[47] during which time Jesus Christ gives Saul His gospel by Divine revelation.[48] Saul then returns to Damascus and resumes preaching in the synagogues.[49] The Jews plot to kill him, but Saul learns of their plan. The governor under King Aretas has the gates of the city guarded so that Saul cannot escape.[50] When Saul learns of this, the believers in Damascus lower him out of a window by a basket during the night through an opening in the wall. Saul flees Damascus safely.[51]

Saul travels south to Jerusalem to meet Peter. The church there is fearful of him, not believing his conversion is genuine. Barnabas, however, believes his conversion is real and introduces Saul to Peter. Barnabas shares Saul's conversion experience with Peter, and Saul is received. Saul stays with Peter for about two weeks (fifteen days to be exact). Saul meets James (the Lord's half-brother) also. Peter and James tell Saul about Jesus' earthly life and sayings.[52] Saul has been a Christian for three years now.[53]

While in Jerusalem, Saul boldly preaches Christ in the synagogues. But the Grecian Jews try to kill him. Saul visits the temple to pray, and the Lord appears to him in a trance. Jesus tells him to leave the city, for the Jews will not receive his testimony. The Lord also adds that He will be sending him far away to the Gentiles.[54] The believers in Jerusalem bring Saul to Caesarea which is 64 miles north of Jerusalem. They send him off by ship to Tarsus, his hometown.

Saul begins traveling throughout the regions of Syria and Cilicia.[55] With the exception of Jerusalem, the churches in Judea have never seen Saul. But they get word that the man who once persecuted the churches is now preaching the faith he once tried to destroy. The churches glorify God for this.[56]

With Saul converted, the persecution ends. The churches in Judea, Galilee, and Samaria enjoy peace and spiritual prosperity. The Twelve continue to travel to the newly founded churches throughout Palestine, encouraging and strengthening them in the Lord.[57]

Peter Travels Through Palestine
A.D. 40-41

Peter makes a general tour of the churches in Western Judea. He visits the church in Lydda and heals a man named Aeneas of the palsy. The church in Lydda grows as a result of the miracle.

Peter then visits Joppa, a town ten miles northwest of Lydda. While there he raises a respected sister in Christ named Tabitha (or Dorcas) from the dead. The church in Joppa grows as a result of the miracle. Peter remains in Joppa for a long time. He resides with Simon the tanner who lives in a house near the sea.[58]

Cornelius, a Roman centurion,[59] is living in the predominantly Gentile city of Caesarea. Cornelius is a "God-fearer." God-fearers are uncircumcised Gentiles who worship the God of Israel. Cornelius is also a man of prayer and benevolence. At 3:00 p.m., he receives a vision of an angel who instructs him to invite Peter to his home.

The next day at noon, Peter is praying on his rooftop. He becomes hungry and falls into a trance. He then receives a vision of a sheet falling from Heaven. The sheet contains many unclean animals. Peter hears a voice saying, "Rise up, kill, and eat...What God has cleansed do not call unclean." The vision occurs three times. (The meaning of the vision is that God will cleanse the Gentiles.)

Not long after the vision ends, three men sent from Cornelius visit Peter. They explain to Peter why they are visiting him, and Peter invites them to be his guests for the evening. The next day Peter, the men Cornelius sent, and six brothers from the church in Joppa head out to Caesarea to meet Cornelius. The trip from Joppa to Caeasarea, a distance of 40 miles, takes two days. (A day's journey on foot is about 20 miles.)

A Church Planted in Caesarea

Peter arrives in Caesarea and is greeted by Cornelius, his household, and a large group of Gentiles. After they exchange stories of how God brought the two men together, Peter preaches Christ. (Mark's Gospel is essentially an expanded version of Peter's message.[60])

While Peter is still preaching, the Gentiles believe on Christ and the Spirit of God falls upon them, causing them to speak in other tongues. The men who accompanied Peter are shocked, because they did not expect God to give His Spirit to Gentiles.

Peter has them all baptized in water. The Gentiles are now added to the Body of Christ! The "unclean" are now part of the Spirit-baptized community! Jew and Gentile no longer exist in the church. The church is one new humanity—including both Jew and Gentile! The first Gentile church is born in Caesarea. The new converts beg Peter to stay with them for a longer time.[61]

Meanwhile, the church in Jerusalem has repopulated itself. Many Jewish priests have become Christians and have been added to the believing community. These ex-priests will make up what is called "the circumcision party." The circumcision party are those brethren in the Jerusalem church who are zealous for the Law of Moses. They believe that Gentiles are unclean and must be circumcised to receive God's favor.

The report that the Gentiles have received the gospel spreads like wildfire all throughout Judea. When Jerusalem hears of it, some of the believers in the church are alarmed and infuriated. (The Law prohibits the fraternization of Jew and Gentile. From their childhood, Jews have been taught never to eat with or touch an unclean Gentile. So in their eyes, what Peter did by visiting and eating with Gentiles was sinful and repulsive.)

When Peter returns to Jerusalem, he is reproved by the circumcision party for fellowshipping with Gentiles. Peter, however, retells the vision of the unclean animals, rehearses the story of his visit to Caesarea and how God supernaturally spoke to him and Cornelius. Peter manages to persuade his fellow Jewish brethren that God has received the Gentiles into the believing community, giving them eternal life also.[62]

ENDNOTES

1. Acts 12:12. This very well may be the same house that Jesus used to keep the Passover meal on the eve of His death (Mark 14:15ff; John 20:19,26).

2. Acts 1:12-15.

3. Matthew 13:55; Mark 6:3.

4. According to tradition, Joseph Barsabbas was one of the 70 that Jesus sent out during His earthly ministry (Luke 10:1ff).

5. Casting lots was a Hebrew custom to obtain the Lord's mind on a matter (Proverbs 16:33). After the Spirit is poured out on the day of Pentecost, we never see the early Christians casting lots to lay hold of God's mind.

6. Acts 1:16-26.

7. Leviticus 23:15-17.

8. The Twelve were already filled inwardly when Christ was resurrected. Today, they are empowered outwardly. The 108 receive both the inward filling and the outward empowering of the Spirit.

9. Acts 2:1-12.

10. 1 Corinthians 12:13; Ephesians 2:11-19.

11. Acts 2:14ff.

12. Acts 2:41-47.

13. Or Mishnaic Hebrew.

14. The message that the Twelve preach is Christ (1 John 1:1-3).

15. Acts 3:11; 5:12.

16. Acts 3.

17. There were two main religious parties in first-century Israel: The Pharisees and Sadducees. The Sadducees controlled the temple establishment. They denied the existence of spirits, angels, the soul, the after-life, and the resurrection. They only observed the Law of Moses (the first five Books of the Old Testament) and ignored the rest. The Pharisees embraced all the Old Testament and believed in spirits, angels, the soul, and the resurrection. They were the sectarian purists, obsessed with strict legalism, especially in respect to Jewish dietary laws and ceremonial cleanliness. Of the 500,000 or so Jewish residents in Palestine, over 6,000 were Pharisees. The Sadducees had their hands on the levers of political power. They were "the establishment" of the day. Sadducees were found among the wealthy landowners and aristocratic high priestly families. Pharisees were made up mostly of artisans and merchants from the middle and lower urban classes.

18. Luke points out the consistent growth of the Jerusalem church throughout Acts. On the birthday of the church, 3,000 are converted (Acts 2:41). The church now has a "multitude" of believers (Acts 4:32). Not long after, it swells to 5,000 men. It has moved from a "multitude" to "multitudes" (Acts 5:14). In a short time following, the number of the believers multiplies greatly (Acts 6:7). With the persecution under Saul, the church dissolves. But 20 years later, it has grown to "myriads" (Acts 21:20).

19. Caiaphas' reign extended from A.D. 18-36. In this period, the high priest no longer achieved his office by blood-line, but by appointment. The high priest of Jesus' day was appointed by Pilate.

20. Barnabas' "land" or "field" refers to medium-sized estates or larger. Unlike what is prescribed in the Law, the Levites during this time could own land.

21. Acts 4.

22. Acts 5:1-11.

23. The school of Hillel was the liberal wing of the Pharisees as opposed to the school of Shammai, which was the conservative wing.

24. Acts 22:3.

25. This was the normal punishment handed out by Jewish courts (Deuteronomy 25:2-4).

26. Acts 5:12-42.

27. The Grecian (Hellenistic) Jews were born outside of Palestine. They speak Greek only and have adopted Greek culture and customs. The Hebraic Jews speak Aramaic or Mishnaic Hebrew only (or Aramaic and Greek) and have adopted Jewish culture and customs. Most Hebraic Jews were born in Palestine.

28. According to Irenaeus (A.D. 180), this man later founded the Nicolaitan party that is condemned in Revelation 2:6,15.

29. Acts 6:1-7.

30. Freedmen are former slaves who have been released. Some of them proved to become wealthy and influential. However, most remained poor and had less security than in their previous life as slaves.

31. Acts 6:14. When Judea became a Roman province in A.D. 6, the jurisdiction for capital offenses was reserved to the Roman governor except in this one case.

32. Mark 14:57ff.

33. In these words are echoes of Jesus' last words to His Father. "Father, into Your hands I commit My spirit" (Luke 23:46 NIV).

34. Again, Stephen echoes the forgiving spirit of Jesus Christ when He too was unjustly slain (Luke 23:34).

35. Acts 6:8–7:60; 8:2.

36. Acts 8:1-4.

37. 1 Corinthians 9:5.

38. Jesus had sown the seed of the gospel in this city almost a decade beforehand. Philip now reaps it (John 4:1-42).

39. The word of Jesus to the Twelve in Acts 1:8 begins to find fulfillment. They are His witnesses in Judea, Samaria, and the utmost parts of the world.

40. A eunuch is a person who has been castrated. Kings were generally accustomed to having eunuchs as guardians of their treasury because they could not be tempted by women.

41. According to Irenaeus (A.D. 180), the eunuch brought the gospel to his own people.

42. Acts 8:5-40.

43. Some scholars, such as Ben Witherington and F.F. Bruce, date Paul's conversion to be A.D. 33 or 34.

44. Acts 9:1-2; 22:5ff; 26:9ff; 1 Corinthians 15:9; Galatians 1:13,15; Philippians 3:6; 1 Timothy 1:13.

45. Acts 9:7; 22:9; 26:12-18.

46. Acts 9:3-22.

47. Arabia does not refer to the sandy desert, but to the Nabataean kingdom and its cities (Petra, Gerasa, Bostra, etc.).

48. Galatians 1:11-18. Paul (Saul) makes clear that his gospel was given to him before he had contact with any of the Twelve apostles.

49. Galatians 1:13-17.

50. 2 Corinthians 11:32-33. King Aretas was king of the Nabataean Arabs. Paul may have done some preaching to the Nabataeans at the end of his stay in Arabia since the governor under Aretas—who was the leader of the Nabataean community—showed hostility to Paul and was hunting him down. It seems that both the governor and the Jews in Damascus plotted to arrest Paul. But when Paul describes the event in 2 Corinthians 11:32, he avoids accusing his own people (as was his custom).

51. Acts 9:23-25; 2 Corinthians 11:32-33.

52. Among the many things that Peter and James spoke to Saul regarding Jesus, they included how and when He appeared to them after His resurrection (1 Corinthians 15:4-7).

53. Galatians 1:18-19. That which Peter shares with Paul about Christ's earthly life and sayings appears in Paul's epistles.

54. Acts 22:17-21.

55. Galatians 1:21; Acts 9:30.

56. Galatians 1:22-24.

57. Acts 9:26-31.

58. Acts 9:32-43.

59. A soldier in charge of 100 men.

60. This is because Mark received his account of Jesus Christ mostly from Peter. In addition, Mark's outline in his Gospel is identical to the outline of Peter's spoken messages in Acts.

61. Acts 10; 11:5-16.

62. Acts 11:1-18.

Chapter 8

The Antioch Chronicle

A.D. 41–A.D. 47

But there were some of them, Cypriot and Cyrenian men, who came to Antioch and began speaking to the Hellenists, proclaiming the good news about the Lord Jesus. The Lord's hand was with them, and a large number who believed turned to the Lord (Acts 11:20-21).

A.D. 41

Some of the Christians who dispersed throughout Palestine make their way to Phoenicia, Cyprus, and a large city in Syria called Antioch. These Christians preach to their fellow Grecian (Hellenistic) Jews in these areas.

Sharpening the Focus: Antioch of Syria is located on the Orontes River and sits 300 miles north of Jerusalem. According to Jewish historian Josephus (A.D. 100), Antioch is the third largest city in the Roman Empire, following Rome and Alexandria. The city is known as "the queen of the East," "Antioch the beautiful," and "the third city of the Empire."

Antioch is the center of political, military, and commercial communication between Rome and the Persian frontier. It is a wealthy city and the only one that has streetlights at this time. Its main east-west street is paved with polished stone and there are colonnades on both sides. Antioch's population is estimated between 300,000 and 500,000. The Jewish population is large and vigorous, standing between 22,000 and 50,000. Nicolas, one of "the seven," was a Jewish proselyte from Antioch. In the years to come, Syrian Antioch will become the cradle of Gentile Christianity.

> Antioch of Syria is typical of all Greco-Roman cities of the first century. It is a pesthole of infectious disease. Sickness is highly visible on the streets. Swollen eyes, skin rashes, and lost limbs are readily seen in public. The city is populated with recent newcomers so it is peopled by strangers. The city is filled with misery, danger, despair, fear, and hatred. The average family lives in filthy and crowded quarters. At least half the children die at birth or during infancy.
>
> Most children lose one parent before reaching maturity. There is intense ethnic antagonism which breeds hatred and fear. This problem is worsened by the constant influx of foreigners. Crime is rampant, and the streets are unsafe at night. Not a few residents are homeless. What Christianity will bring to this city and all others is a *new culture* capable of making life in Greco-Roman cities more tolerable. The community of Jesus Christ—the church—will bring joy, hope, charity, a sense of family, and social solidarity to such cruel conditions.

A Church Planted in Antioch of Syria

However, some of the dispersed Christians—those originally from Cyprus and Cyrene—preach the gospel to the Gentiles in Antioch. A Cypriot named Mnason is among them.[1] The Lord's hand is with these Christians, and a great number of Greeks believe the gospel. There is now a community expressing Jesus Christ in Antioch. The church in Antioch is quickly becoming a church full of Law-free Gentiles.

The church in Jerusalem gets wind of the news concerning the Lord's work in Antioch. The believers in Jerusalem send Barnabas, who is originally from Cyprus, to supervise and direct the Christian advance in Antioch. (The church in Jerusalem has great confidence in Barnabas.)

When Barnabas comes to Antioch, he is overjoyed by what he sees God doing among the Gentiles. He immediately begins encouraging the new church which is growing rapidly.[2]

A.D. 42

Saul of Tarsus is still in his hometown in Cilicia. While there, he has a profound spiritual experience. It is so striking that he is not sure if he is taken out of his body or not. All he knows is that in some way he ascends to the third Heaven[3] and hears and sees things that are unlawful for a man to repeat.[4]

The Antioch Christians

The church in Antioch has grown so large that Barnabas can no longer care for it on his own. He remembers Saul and recalls that Saul speaks Greek, that he is from the Hellenistic city of Tarsus, and that the Lord called him to minister to the Gentiles.

Barnabas heads out to Tarsus to search for Saul. After searching the city, he finds Saul and brings him back to Antioch. The two men spend a year strengthening the church there. Barnabas is doing most of the ministry, and Saul is an apprentice to him.

In Antioch, Saul lives with Simon of Cyrene (also called Simeon), his wife, and his two sons, Rufus and Alexander. Simon's wife cares for Saul and acts like a mother to him. (Simon carried the cross of Christ.)[5] The believers are first designated "Christians" (Christ's people) in Antioch. They do not call themselves Christians, nor is this name given to them by the Jews (for the Jews do not believe that Jesus is the Christ—the Messiah). It is rather given to them by their Greek-speaking neighbors. The reason? The believers are constantly talking about their Lord, just as Jesus constantly talked about His Father. The Christians in Antioch are consumed with Jesus Christ, and out of the abundance of their hearts their mouths speak.[6] The new movement is also called "The Way"—a term the Christians use for the way of salvation and the way of life.[7] In Palestine, the Christians are known as "Nazarenes."[8]

There are two men in the Antioch church who will play a key role in the story: Luke and Titus.[9] Titus will one day become an apostolic worker (church planter), but only after he has had time to develop spiritually in the church. Luke is a Gentile itinerant (traveling) physician who plies his trade in places like Troas and Philippi.[10] Titus is Luke's younger brother.[11]

The Coming Famine
Summer 43

Prophets from the Jerusalem church pay Antioch a visit. One of them named Agabus prophesies of a great famine that will encompass the entire Roman world.[12] The Jerusalem church is in poverty and will be devastated by the coming famine.

Upon hearing this, the believers in Antioch begin laying up a collection of money to relieve their brethren in Jerusalem. Each person gives according to his ability, in proportion to his prosperity. The church selects Barnabas and Saul to bring the money to the elders in Jerusalem.

King Herod Agrippa (grandson of Herod the Great) is ruling over Judea at this time. The church in Jerusalem is growing again. And the Jewish establishment feels threatened.[13]

James the Apostle Is Martyred
April 44

During the season of Unleavened Bread, King Herod seeks to gain favor with the Jews. Since the Jews in Jerusalem hate the Christians, Herod unmercifully executes James, the son of Zebedee and brother of John. James is beheaded, and is the first of the Twelve to be martyred.[14] Upon seeing that James' death pleases the Jews, Herod takes Peter into custody. Peter is heavily guarded by four squads of four men during the various watches of the night. Herod's plan is to put Peter on public trial after Passover.

The believers in Jerusalem fervently pray for Peter's release. The Lord hears their prayers and supernaturally delivers Peter from prison by the hand of an angel. Upon his release, Peter heads to the house of Mary (the mother of John Mark). A large group of believers is praying when Peter arrives.

When Peter knocks on the door, Rhoda answers. Upon hearing Peter's voice, she runs and tells the believers that Peter is at the door. They do not believe her, however. Peter is let in and the believers are amazed. Peter gives a report of the miracle and asks them to tell James (the Lord's half-brother) and the rest of the church. He then leaves. The next day, in the morning, Herod learns that Peter has escaped. He then orders that the guards responsible for watching Peter be executed. Herod leaves Judea and heads off to Caesarea. While there, he tries to put out a few political fires with the people of Tyre and Sidon.

August 1, 44

Herod delivers an oration to the people of Caesarea from his kingly throne. He is draped in a royal robe of silver that glitters spectacularly when the sunbeams hit it. As he speaks, the public utters out: "You are more than a mortal; you are a god!" Herod does not rebuke the people, but accepts their impious flattery. Immediately, the angel of the Lord strikes him down. Herod complains of intestinal pains and is removed from the crowds. He suffers with stomach pains for five days until he dies.[15] The cause of death is intestinal worms that eat his insides.[16]

Jerusalem Gets Relief From Antioch

Despite the renewed persecution, the church in Jerusalem is still growing. Saul and Barnabas leave Antioch and head off to Jerusalem to deliver the relief fund. They take Titus with them as a Gentile representative of the Antioch church.[17] The journey from Jerusalem to Antioch is approximately 300 miles. When they arrive, Saul, Barnabas, and Titus graciously hand the collection over to the Jerusalem elders.

The three men have a private meeting with Peter, James, and John (the pillars of the Jerusalem church). In this meeting, Saul and Barnabas give a report about God's work among the Gentiles in Antioch. Saul and Barnabas also share with them their burden to bring the gospel to the Gentiles.

Some "false brethren" of the circumcision party are also present. They are undercover agents who infiltrate the meeting with an agenda to put the Gentiles in Antioch under Mosaic Law. Since Titus is not circumcised, they make him an issue.[18]

Peter, James, and John are unconvinced by the circumcision party and approve of Saul's Law-free gospel to the Gentiles. The three apostles give Saul and Barnabas "the right hand of fellowship" and make a gentleman's agreement. They agree that Saul and Barnabas' chief sphere of ministry will be to the Gentile world while Peter's chief sphere of ministry will be to the Jewish world.

The three Jerusalem apostles merely request that Saul and Barnabas continue to remember the poor saints in Jerusalem—a request that was already in Saul's heart. (Later, Saul will take up a collection from all the Gentile churches that he will plant to try and relieve the chronic poverty of the Jerusalem church.)[19]

Saul, Barnabas, and Titus head back home to Antioch of Syria. They take with them Barnabas' young cousin, John Mark.[20] ("John" is his Jewish name while "Mark" is his Roman name. He is the same Mark that authored the Gospel of Mark.)[21]

A Special Prayer Meeting
Spring 47

The church in Antioch is about seven years old. There is a prayer meeting, and five men from the church are present. These men are prophets and teachers, and they are fasting and ministering unto the Lord.[22] They are:

- Simeon called Niger (Niger is his Latin surname indicating that he is of dark complexion. He is also known as Simon of Cyrene. He carried the cross of Christ.)[23]
- Lucius of Cyrene
- Manaen (An aristocrat. Probably the foster brother of Herod Antipas who was the youngest son of Herod the Great.)
- Barnabas
- Saul

Barnabas and Saul Are Sent

Just as the Father called and sent the Son, and just as the Son called and sent the Twelve, the Holy Spirit calls and sends Barnabas and Saul to the work of planting churches.[24] Like the Twelve, they are now "sent ones"—apostles.[25] But their sending has not been without preparation. Barnabas has lived in the experience of the church for seventeen years (ten years in Jerusalem and seven in Antioch). He was also trained by the Twelve. Saul has lived in the experience of the church in Antioch for five years. He was trained by Barnabas.[26]

The other three brothers lay hands on Barnabas and Saul on behalf of the Antioch church, sending them out to the work.[27]

ENDNOTES

1. Acts 21:16.

2. Acts 11:19-24.

3. The first heaven is the sky that contains the visible clouds. The second heaven is the atmosphere beyond the clouds. The third Heaven is the spiritual invisible realm where God dwells.

4. 2 Corinthians 12:1-4.

5. Mark 15:21; Romans 16:13; Acts 13:1.

6. Acts 11:26.

7. Acts 9:2; 19:9,23; 22:4; 24:14,22; also 16:17; 18:25-26.

8. Acts 24:5.

9. That Titus is from Antioch is a natural inference from Galatians 2:1-3. Tradition says that Luke is from Antioch, Syria.

10. Colossians 4:14; Acts 16:10ff. When Luke uses the "we" passages in Acts 16, 20, 21, 27, and 28, it is because he is present. That Luke is Gentile is strongly implied by Colossians 4:10-11,14.

11. This is a common view held by scholars. It also explains why Luke never mentions Titus in the Book of Acts.

12. The famine eventually took place under the reign of Claudius. Dio Cassius' history records famine conditions in Rome at the beginning of Claudius' rule and in other parts of the Empire during the years A.D. 41–54. Historically, Judea suffered famine between A.D. 45–48.

13. Acts 11:27-30.

14. Eusebius (A.D. 320) preserves the tradition that the guard who watched James in prison was so impressed with his witness that he professed himself a Christian and was beheaded along with him.

15. This account comes from the Jewish historian Josephus as well as Luke's account.

16. Acts 12:1-23. The first twelve chapters of Acts are dominated by Peter. The remainder of Acts shifts its focus to Paul.

17. Galatians 2:1.

18. Galatians 2:1-5.

19. Galatians 2:6-10.

20. Colossians 4:10.

21. Acts 12:24-25.

22. Acts 13:1-2.

23. Mark 15:21.

24. John 20:21; Acts 13:2. For a discussion on the word *work* as it is used in the NT, see my book *So You Want to Start a House Church?*, Chapter 2.

25. Paul and Barnabas are called "apostles" in Acts 14:4,14.

26. For a discussion of how God raises up and sends apostolic workers to plant churches, see *So You Want to Start a House Church?*, Chapter 3.

27. Acts 13:3.

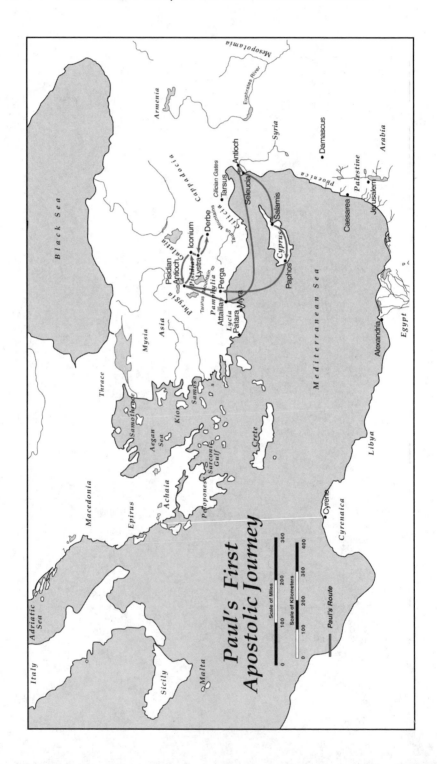

Paul's First Apostolic Journey

CHAPTER 9

THE GALATIAN CHRONICLE

A.D. 47–A.D. 50

They continued their journey from Perga and reached Antioch in Pisidia. On the Sabbath day they went into the synagogue and sat down (Acts 13:14).

PREVIEW OF PAUL'S FIRST APOSTOLIC JOURNEY

Time: 2 years
Years: A.D. 47-49
Miles Traveled: 1200 miles
Churches Planted: (4) Pisidian Antioch, Iconium, Lystra, and Derbe
Time Planted:
Pisidian Antioch = 3-5 months
Iconium = 3-5 months
Lystra = 3-5 months
Derbe = 3-5 months

Barnabas and Saul set out from Antioch, Syria. Barnabas takes the lead role. They take John Mark along with them to be their attendant. John Mark carries some of the luggage and other necessary items. He is also an eyewitness to the resurrection of Christ.[1] This will come in handy when the two men preach the gospel in foreign lands.

The three men head to a seaport in Seleucia (sixteen miles from Antioch). From there, they sail off to the Island of Cyprus (60 miles offshore from Antioch). Cyprus is Barnabas' native land.

A Visit to Cyprus
Spring 47

Sharpening the Focus: Cyprus belongs to the province of Cilicia. The principal export of Cyprus is copper, from which it derives its

its name. (Barnabas probably sold a copper field when he pooled his money to help the Jerusalem church seventeen years ago.) Cyprus stretches 140 miles from east to west. It is an island made up mostly of Greeks. Yet it has a large Jewish population.

Barnabas, Saul, and John Mark come to a town in east Cyprus called Salamis. Salamis has a large Jewish community and several synagogues. Barnabas and Saul begin preaching in the synagogues. This will become a common practice of Saul. He will bring the gospel "to the Jew first, then to the Gentile."

The three men traverse the island from east to west. They preach in the synagogues and strengthen the churches that have been transplanted during the Jerusalem dispersion.[2]

When they come to the west side of the island, they stop in a town called Paphos (also called New Paphos). Paphos is the administrative capital of Cyprus. There, Barnabas and Saul are tied to a pillar, whipped[3]—receiving the "forty less one" beating[4]—and imprisoned.

The governor (also called proconsul) of Cyprus, Sergius Paulus, invites the men to speak to him about their religion. As Barnabas and Saul share Christ with the governor, his personal sorcerer Bar-Jesus (also called Elymas, which is Semitic for "sorcerer") rudely and deliberately interrupts the men. In response, Saul rebukes Bar-Jesus and the Lord's hand comes upon him. Bar-Jesus is blinded! Beholding this miraculous event, Sergius Paulus becomes a Christian. The governor is Barnabas and Saul's first recorded Gentile convert.[5]

Sergius Paulus has relatives in a land called Pisidia in the province of Galatia. He encourages Barnabas and Saul to visit Pisidia to share Christ with them.[6] So the three men head due north, toward Pisidia.[7]

Sailing to South Galatia
Summer 47

The men set sail along the Mediterranean Sea from Paphos to Perga of Pamphylia. At this point Saul takes the lead in the journey.[8] He also uses his Greco-Roman name, Paul (Paulos) instead of his Jewish name, Saul.

Sharpening the Focus: Passenger ships do not exist in the first century. One has to find a merchant sailing ship or a cargo ship that has space. The bigger the ship, the safer the travel. The biggest ships are grain ships. Sailing is quite inexpensive. Except for emergencies, no sailing is to be done during the winter months due to the inclement weather. The seas are treacherous from November 11 to March 10. The prime time for sailing is May 27-September 14. March 10-May 26 and September 14-November 11 are hazardous, but still sailable. No matter what time of the year it is, pagan sailors always wait for an omen from the gods before they set out to sea. A sacrifice is typically made beforehand and the entrails of the animal are read to determine if sailing is favorable. (The Alexandrian ship that Paul will take to get to Rome will have attached to it the figureheads of the twin gods, Castor and Pullox, whom the pagans believe provide protection from storms—Acts 28:11!)

In the region that Paul and Barnabas are now traveling, the Etesian winds can be a problem. The Etesian winds are prevailing northerly monsoonal winds that appear in the summer and early fall. The winds flow into the Aegean Sea and into the eastern Mediterranean, from north to south.

Antioch of Pisidia is 3600 feet above sea level. The men must cross over the Taurus Mountains to get there. This is a very dangerous journey. The roads are not safe, and they abound with robbers. The rivers in this area are also known to overflow easily, causing many to drown. When Paul will write of "dangers from robbers and dangers from rivers" in 2 Corinthians, he is undoubtedly speaking of the journey from Perga to Pisidia. The ordinary rate of travel by foot in the first century is 20 miles a day. Therefore, the journey from Perga to Pisidia will take approximately ten days.

Paul and Barnabas undoubtedly had to stop at the local tavern inns on their journey. Well-to-do Romans avoid these inns at all cost. Inns are noted for their filthy sleeping quarters, adulterated wine, extortionate innkeepers, gamblers, thieves, and prostitutes, not to mention their bug-infested beds.

The journey from Paphos to Perga is accompanied by a shipwreck.[9] The shipwreck, coupled with the bandits who haunted the Taurus Mountains, greatly discourage John Mark from continuing on the journey. He is also disturbed that Paul is now the leader of the apostolic mission, instead of his cousin Barnabas, and Paul is prepared to preach outside the synagogue to Gentiles with greater freedom than Mark had anticipated. All this causes John Mark to get homesick, so he heads back to Jerusalem. Paul views John Mark's departure as unfaithful abandonment.[10] In addition to all these setbacks, Paul is sick.[11]

A Church Planted in Antioch of Pisidia

When Paul and Barnabas come to the land of Pisidia, they stop at a Roman colony called Antioch—Antioch of Pisidia.[12]

Sharpening the Focus: The Romans divided the political province of South Galatia into the following regions: Pisidia, Lyconia, and Phrygia. Antioch of Pisidia is located in what today is west central Turkey. It is a Roman colony and belongs to Phrygia rather than to Pisidia. Its technical name is "Antioch-near-Pisidia." The city is adorned with buildings devoted to the imperial cult.

Pisidian Antioch is the civil and administrative center of the Galatian province. The intellectual section of the city is Greek, while the majority of the population is Phrygian. The Phrygians are an unwarlike people who have been subject for centuries to other races. In fact, "Phrygian" is a disparaging slave name. Greek as well as Phrygian are spoken in Antioch. There is a well-established minority of Jews living there, but it is not large since there is only one synagogue in the city.

Paul and Barnabas visit the local synagogue in Pisidian Antioch. After the Law and the Prophets are read, there is a time for guests to give a word of exhortation to the congregation. The synagogue officials ask Paul and Barnabas if they would like to address the congregation. Paul responds and preaches Jesus Christ. His message is virtually the same message that Stephen brought the day that he was stoned.[13] Paul heard that message firsthand and remembered it.

The audience is made up of Jews, Jewish proselytes, and God-fearers. Jews are born Israelites. They have been circumcised on the eighth day after their birth. Their circumcision shows that they have a covenant with God.

Proselytes are Gentiles who have converted over to Judaism. They have been circumcised. They have also been ceremonially bathed, have offered a sacrifice, and have vowed to keep the Law of Moses. Proselytes have become complete Jews. As such, they are full members of the synagogue.

God-fearers are Gentiles who follow the God of Israel. But they are not circumcised. Therefore, they are not full members of the synagogue.

When the synagogue service ends, the people beg Paul to continue his message the next Sabbath. Many of the Jews and proselytes follow Paul and Barnabas, asking them questions. Paul and Barnabas urge them to persevere in God's grace. News about Paul's message that the Messiah has come spreads throughout the entire city.

When the next Sabbath rolls around, almost the whole city pours into the synagogue to hear Paul preach! This incites the Jewish leaders to jealousy. They begin to revile and contradict Paul as he speaks. They also point to the fact that Paul is sick in an attempt to discount his message. (In the mind of a Jew, being sick is a visible sign that God's hand is against you.)

Paul and Barnabas leave the synagogue and begin preaching to the Gentiles. The Gentiles receive Paul as a messenger of God, despite his sickness.[14] Paul's message spreads throughout the entire region.

In a few months' time, the local Jews go to the Gentile civic authorities and stir up the noble God-fearing women against the two apostolic workers. As a result, Paul and Barnabas are legally banished from the district. They are beaten with birch rods as well. (A formal beating was part of the banishing process.) The two men shake the dust off their feet against the city and leave.

When Paul and Barnabas depart, they leave a church in Pisidian Antioch—a community that expresses Jesus Christ. The church is mostly Gentile, and the new converts are filled with joy and the Holy Spirit.[15]

A Church Planted in Iconium
A.D. 47–48

As the blood dries on their backs, Paul and Barnabas travel 90 miles southeast to the frontier town of Iconium. This is roughly a five-day walk. The two men take the Roman military road called the Via Sebaste, which will eventually lead them to Lystra and Derbe.[16]

Iconium is a Greek city. Phrygian and Greek are spoken here. As is their custom, Paul and Barnabas visit the synagogue and preach Christ boldly in utter dependence on their Lord. Their message is so effective that a great multitude believes, both Jews and Greeks. The Word they bring is also confirmed by signs and wonders.

Unfortunately, the Antioch experience is repeated in Iconium. The unbelieving Jews become jealous and agitated. They begin to persuade the people against the two apostles. The city is divided. Some side with the Jews; others side with Paul and Barnabas.

There is a plot afoot by some Jews, Gentiles, and rulers of the city to stone the two men. When Paul and Barnabas get wind of it, they leave the city, escaping the mob violence. The two men head toward the Lyconian cities of Lystra and Derbe as well as the surrounding countryside where they continue to preach Christ. As they depart Iconium, they leave behind the Body of Christ—a community that expresses God's life and nature in the city.[17]

A Church Planted in Lystra

Paul and Barnabas take the Via Sebaste and travel eighteen miles southwest to a Roman colony called Lystra.[18] Lystra is a very primitive town that is built on a small hill. The old Lyconian language is still spoken here, as well as Greek. Since Lystra is a Roman colony, the language of the courts and the Roman soldiers is Latin. There is no synagogue, indicating there are hardly any Jews present.

There is an old legend that says that the Greek gods Zeus and Hermes once visited Lystra.[19] They appeared as humans looking for a place to stay. After they were rejected by the people, an elderly couple took the gods into their home. The gods turned their home into a palace. That palace became the temple of Zeus.[20]

Paul heals a lame man who was crippled from birth. After beholding the miracle, the Lyconians think that Paul is Hermes and Barnabas is Zeus and that the gods are returning to Lystra. (They call Paul Hermes because he is the leading speaker.)

Thinking the men are gods, the priest of Zeus, whose temple sits in front of the city, brings oxen and wreaths to the city gates, intending to offer a sacrifice to the two apostles. When Paul and Barnabas hear what is going on, they tear their clothes and run out among the crowd. They tell the people that they are mere mortals and command them to stop sacrificing to them. Despite their attempt, Paul and Barnabas have trouble persuading the Lyconians to not offer sacrifice to them.

Not long after this, Jews from Pisidian Antioch and Iconium descend on the city. They incite the crowds against Paul and Barnabas. The Lyconians suddenly turn on the men. They stone Paul and drag him out of the city, leaving him for dead.[21] A young man watches this, a convert from Lystra whose name is Timothy (also called Timotheus).[22] Both his mother, Eunice, and his grandmother, Lois, are converted.[23] They are Jews, but Timothy's father is Greek.[24]

The believers in Lystra gather around Paul, and he rises up—healed! Yet the stoning has left wounds on his body that will turn into scars. From henceforth, Paul will bear the marks of his Lord in his physical body.[25]

Paul and Barnabas go back into the city to get their belongings. The next day they leave, but they leave behind a community of people who are expressing God's nature in Lystra.[26] There is now a church—the Body of Jesus Christ—living in the city.

A Church Planted in Derbe

The two apostles head 60 miles southeast to a tiny frontier town called Derbe. In Derbe, they preach the gospel of Christ. Many disciples are made as a result. A convert is made in the town whose name is Gaius.[27] There is now a church in Derbe—a community expressing God's nature.

After preaching the gospel in Derbe, Paul and Barnabas retrace their steps. Despite the fact that they have been driven out of these cities, they revisit Lystra, Iconium, and Pisidian Antioch. In each city, they meet with the church briefly to strengthen, encourage, and warn them of the trials that lie ahead. After prayer and fasting, the apostles identify the older men in each church that have matured the most. They acknowledge these men as "elders."[28] After commending each church to the Lord Jesus Christ, Paul and Barnabas depart.[29]

Sharpening the Focus: If we take into account their travel time, Paul and Barnabas spend only three to five months planting each Galatian church. This is a pattern that holds throughout Paul's entire ministry. He will spend a short amount of time laying a solid foundation for an infant church. Then he will abandon it for a long period of time without human headship or designated leadership.

Two years will pass before Paul will return to see the Galatian believers. Most of the converts in South Galatia are heathen Gentiles. There are some God-fearers and some Jews among them. The Gentiles were once unwashed pagans. They come from a background that is racked with superstition, false gods, and immorality. The God-fearers are Gentiles who attended the synagogue to hear about the God of Israel. The Jews are the clean-cut, cultured, morally-conscious members of the church.

By conservative estimates, over fifty percent of these converts are slaves. A large number are freedmen, which are former slaves.

There may be a few believers who are part of the Roman army. And there may be a few merchants.

In the Greco-Roman world, slaves were not distinguished by any physical or educational differences from the general population. Most were used in manufacturing and household maintenance. The most common route of slavery was lost wars; piracy was also a major way that people were made slaves. Failing to pay personal debts was another. Children of slaves remained slaves, and even free children were sometimes sold into slavery, especially females. "Freedmen" consisted of former slaves who did not possess full rights as citizens. Most of them are extremely poor since they have less security than they did in their previous lives as slaves.

The new converts in South Galatia do not have any Bibles. The NT has not been written yet. Possibly a Jew in one of the four churches has one or two scrolls of some OT Book. But it is highly doubtful that any of the churches in South Galatia have a complete OT. Yet even if every convert had an entire Bible, it would profit them little. For only five to ten percent of the population in the Roman Empire are literate. (An estimated ninety percent of the Empire is functionally illiterate. In a few Hellenistic cities, the literacy rate may be as high as twenty to thirty percent. But in the Western provinces of the Roman Empire, it is unlikely that the literacy rate is as high as five percent.) Letter writers, stenographers, occasional poets, and legal scribes make up only four percent of the population at best. Those who can write become farsighted by the age of forty. Thus they will need an amanuensis (a secretary that serves as a professional scribe) to pen their letters. For this reason, Paul needed an amanuensis to write his epistles (e.g., Romans 16:22). Yet with his own hand he would sign the last part of each letter to confirm its authenticity (Galatians 6:11; 2 Thessalonians 3:17; 1 Corinthians 16:21). Sometimes he would add a marginal note with his own hand (Philemon 19). Trusted amaneunses had great freedom to shape the form, style, and even the content of an author's letter.

The poverty among many of the Galatians is daunting. Many of the freedmen in the church live on the borders of human survival. They will seek to find work every day in the marketplace.

When they work, they are paid a day's wage (one Roman denarius). This will buy barely enough food to feed their families. The normal diet of a lower class person in the first century is veggies, bread, wine, olives, fish, and fruit. Meat is eaten on very rare and special occasions. Higher class folks had meat more frequently.

In the Roman colonies, the towns are built according to the pattern of Rome (more on that later). In short, they are dirty, smelly, and unsafe. Because of these conditions, many of the people are racked with disease and malnutrition. The average life expectancy for a male is 45. The average life expectancy for a female is 38. (Of all humans born in the Empire, half die before age five.) Women usually marry in their early teens and raise families until they have passed child-bearing age. Very little birth control is practiced. Twenty-five percent of babies do not survive their first year. Three of every ten Jewish children die before the age of eighteen. The number is higher among the Gentiles. Baby girls are sometimes "exposed" (abandoned in remote places to die) if their parents are too poor to care for them.

For most of the population, first-century Galatia is a thankless, loveless, horrible place to live. This is the world into which two apostolic workers from Syrian Antioch come to establish the church of Jesus Christ. Keep in mind that these new Galatian churches are surrounded by Gentile immorality and idolatry. Also, there are Jews in their towns who hate the new faith.

In the face of these insurmountable problems, Paul and Barnabas spend only three to five months with these people. The apostles tell them about Jesus Christ and then leave them on their own. After their brief revisiting trip, the new Christians in Galatia will not see the hair of an apostle for almost two years. But the gospel that Paul and Barnabas preach will be rich and high enough to cause the Galatian churches to survive without any outside help. What Paul and Barnabas preach cause these once heathen, superstitious, selfish, miserable Gentiles to fall in love with one another, to sing, to smile, and to glow with the joy of Jesus Christ.

How did these two men from Antioch of Syria pull off such a thing? It is because they stood in the lineage that stretches back to the dateless past. Like the Twelve before them, they were called, trained, and sent. And they preach an indwelling Christ that will sustain them through the pressures of life.

The churches of Galatia are classless societies where social distinctions are erased. Jews and Gentiles, slave and free, rich and poor no longer exist. The believers see themselves as part of the same family, part of a new race, and part of a new colony from the heavenly realm. They eat together, work together, greet each other with a holy kiss, raise their children together, take care of one another, and bury one another. It is this joy and love that the Galatian Christians have one for another that will shake the Roman Empire to its very foundations.

A.D. 49

From Pisidia Antioch, Paul and Barnabas return to Pamphylia where they preached Christ in Perga. They head down to the plain of Attalia on the coast of the Pamphylian Gulf and sail back to Antioch of Syria where they were initially sent out. In Antioch, the two men gather the church together and give a report of all that God has done. Paul and Barnabas rest in the church of Syrian Antioch for about a year.[30]

Meanwhile, back in Rome, Emperor Claudius issues a decree expelling all the Jews from the "Eternal City" (Rome). According to the historian Seutonius, the Jews are rioting over their various views about Christ.[31] Since Christianity is viewed as a sect of Judaism in the eyes of the Greeks and Romans, all Jews—including Christian and non-Christian—are forced to leave the city. Many of the banished Jews flee to the Greek city of Corinth. A Roman Jew named Aquila and his wife Priscilla are among them.[32] Because Rome has expelled all Jews, Gentiles in all the Roman colonies throughout the Empire regard Jews with even greater suspicion and disfavor than they had before.

Peter Visits Antioch

Peter pays the church in Syrian Antioch a visit. While he is there, he enjoys table-fellowship with the Gentile believers. When the church in Jerusalem discovers that Peter is eating with Gentiles, some of the circumcision party in Jerusalem head to Antioch to visit Peter.

The circumcision party arrives in Antioch with approval letters from James (the Lord's half-brother). The members of the circumcision party are legalists. They are Judaizers—outrageously zealous to keep the Jewish customs and the Law of Moses and to persuade others to do the same. When they arrive in Antioch, Paul is not present.

The Judaizers persuade Peter to no longer enjoy table-fellowship with his Gentile brethren. They tell Peter the following: "We in Jerusalem have heard that you are habitually having table-fellowship with Gentiles. This is causing a huge scandal to our more conservative brethren in the church. It is also becoming common knowledge outside the church, and it is seriously hindering our attempts to evangelize our fellow Jews. More seriously, your actions are putting the other apostles in Jerusalem in danger, since the militant Jews in Jerusalem view any fraternization with Gentiles to be the conduct of traitors."[33]

Fearful of offending his brethren in Jerusalem, Peter begins to eat exclusively with the Jews. The rest of the Jews in Antioch follow suit. Even Barnabas, who had originally come to Antioch from Jerusalem, stops eating with the Gentiles. When Paul returns and takes note of the situation, he is angered and publicly rebukes Peter for his hypocrisy.[34]

The Judaizers Visit Galatia

Peter returns to Jerusalem and shares the incident with some in the church. He also gives the church a report on the new Gentile churches that Paul and Barnabas have planted in South Galatia. Upon hearing this, some of the Judaizers in Jerusalem head out to Galatia and visit all four churches that Paul and Barnabas planted. The Judaizers are headed up by one unnamed man.[35]

Paul will later refer to this man as his "thorn in the flesh." On three separate occasions, Paul will ask God to remove this "thorn" from his life. The Lord will respond by saying, "My grace is sufficient for you, for My power is made perfect in weakness."[36] That is, the Lord chooses not to remove the thorn from Paul's life, but He will deliver Paul through all the suffering that it will bring him.[37] The thorn—this unnamed Judaizer who will seek to destroy Paul's work—is given to Paul to keep him humble amid the glorious revelation of Christ that he has received.[38]

When the Judaizers arrive in South Galatia, they introduce themselves as brothers from the Jerusalem church. They tell the new converts in Galatia the following:

- Jerusalem is the center of God's work on earth. The twelve apostles are the only authority for what the true gospel is, and they were commissioned by Christ Himself. Paul did not come from Jerusalem, and he was not commissioned by Christ.

- Paul visited Jerusalem shortly after his conversion and spent some time with the apostles there. The apostles instructed him in the basic principles of the gospel and authorized him to preach the gospel he had learned from them. But when he left Jerusalem and returned to Cilicia, Paul modified his gospel to make it more acceptable to Gentiles.

- Paul's gospel is deficient. The Jerusalem leaders believe in the God-given practice of circumcision and observing the Law and the traditions. These are the "hard" parts of the gospel. Because Paul is a man-pleaser, he is preaching a gospel that omits these parts. This Law-free gospel that he proclaims is not supported by the apostles or the Jerusalem church. Believing in Jesus coupled with obeying the Law of Moses justifies and sanctifies a man before God.

- Peter is the chief apostle among the Twelve. Paul had the arrogance to rebuke the apostle Peter to his face! This proves that Paul is a freelancer who is engaging in an independent work apart from the ministry of the Twelve.

- Paul is inconsistent in his views. While he does not preach circumcision to the Gentiles, he preaches it to the Jews. Paul is a trimmer. He adapts his gospel to his environment.

When the Judaizers leave, the Galatian converts are troubled and confused. Some of them depart from the gospel that Paul gave them and seek to be justified by the Law. Some in the church write a letter to Paul asking him why he failed to tell them the "whole gospel," which includes circumcision. Paul, who is still in Antioch, Syria, receives the letter from the Galatian churches. The news from Galatia both angers and perplexes him.[39]

PAUL WRITES GALATIANS

Year: A.D. 49

From: Antioch of Syria

To: The churches in South Galatia: Pisidian Antioch, Iconium, Lystra, and Derbe (these churches are between 1-2 years old)

Provocation: This is the first piece of Christian literature ever penned. The letter is a monumental statement against legalism. Paul answers every argument that the Judaizers used to persuade the Galatians into following the Law of Moses. Galatians is the Magna Carta of the Christian faith. Justification and sanctification are by grace through faith and not by the works of the Law. In this letter, Paul will connect with the Phrygian slaves who populate the Galatian churches. He will use the word "slave" (or its derivative) a total of sixteen times. Many of his metaphors contrast with freedom: "bondage," "confinement," "custodianship," "minor child," and "slavery." Further, Paul will remind the Galatians that they are free from all Law and are holy in Christ without blemish in His sight. In Paul's zeal to preserve the Law-free gospel of Jesus Christ, he writes this letter using bitter metaphors and scathing indictments against the Judaizers. (Example: Paul describes circumcision as being "severed" from Christ and adds his wish that those who insist on circumcision "mutilate" themselves!) It is evident that Paul is angry when writing this letter, for he omits the thanksgiving prayer that marks all of his other letters. Paul is confident that the Galatians will receive the letter and "adopt no other view."

Stop and read Galatians

Sharpening the Focus: Most letters are written on sheets of papyrus. (Those who are too poor to afford papyrus write on broken pieces of pottery called *ostraca*.) Papyrus is a light and tough material made from the stalks of the papyrus plant woven and pressed together. A normal sheet is about the same size as a standard sheet of American paper. For longer documents, the papyrus sheets are glued side-by-side on a stick to form a roll (also called a scroll). Once the scroll has been written upon, it is rolled up and tied with pieces of thread. One roll is called a volume (from the Latin *volumen*, "something rolled up") and is typically 35 feet long. (Authors write to fit volumes. Luke will produce a two-volume work called *Luke-Acts*.) Important documents are normally sealed with hot wax on top of the threads. Then a seal is placed on the scroll to reserve its contents for its proper recipient.

Parchment is also used for letter writing (see 2 Timothy 4:13). Parchment is made from animal skins and is more expensive than papyrus. While most or all of the New Testament authors will use scrolls, a few of them may use codices (plural for codex, a book with pages bound together in the modern style). Writers use a reed pen and black ink that is made of soot, gum, and water. Words are usually written in all capital (*uncial*) letters. Word divisions, punctuation marks, chapters and verses are all lacking in the original writings (these will be added to the NT by editors much later). Ordinary people cannot use the imperial postal system. Thus they must rely on messengers who can deliver their letters to their recipients. Paul's letters (as well as the rest of the NT) are written in *Koine* Greek—the common trade language of the Roman world used by the masses, the merchants, and the marketplace.

The Jerusalem Council
A.D. 50

Back in Antioch of Syria, there is a full-scale debate between the Judaizers from Jerusalem and Paul and Barnabas over the matter of circumcision. The Judaizers insist that the Gentile believers must be circumcised and keep the Law of Moses to be saved. Paul and Barnabas vehemently disagree.

To resolve the matter, the Antioch church sends Paul and Barnabas (and some other men) to Jerusalem to find out if the Judaizers represent the voice of the twelve apostles, the elders, and the entire Jerusalem church.[40]

As the two men journey south, they give a report to the saints in Phoenicia and Samaria about God's work among the Gentiles. The believers in those regions rejoice at the news.

Paul and Barnabas arrive in Jerusalem and are welcomed by the church, the apostles, and the elders. The two men give a report about God's work among the Gentiles. But some of the circumcision party stand up and protest that the Gentiles must be circumcised and keep the Law of Moses. A debate ensues.

Peter speaks and argues that the Gentiles do not have to keep the Law or be circumcised. Salvation is by faith alone. The congregation falls silent. Paul and Barnabas then begin to rehearse all the signs and wonders that God did through them among the Gentiles, which confirmed their gospel of grace.

James (the Lord's half-brother) speaks and summarizes Peter's argument. Agreeing with Peter, he concludes that to help the Gentiles and Jews get along, the Gentiles should observe the following stipulations: They should abstain from food sacrificed to idols, from fornication, from strangled animals (animals with undrained blood), and from eating blood. No other burden should be laid upon the Gentiles.

James' suggestion is accepted and received by the whole church. The decision is reached by the consensus of the church, and the Holy Spirit stands with it.

The church in Jerusalem decides to write a letter stating these prohibitions for the Gentile Christians to read. The whole church, the Twelve, and the Jerusalem elders select two of their prophets to go to Antioch with Paul and Barnabas to authenticate the letter. The two prophets are Judas Barsabbas and Silas (also called Silvanus).

Paul, Barnabas, Judas, and Silas make their way back to Antioch, Syria and deliver the letter to the Antioch church. The letter is read and the Antioch believers rejoice and are greatly encouraged. Judas and Silas stay in Antioch for a time, encouraging and strengthening the church. When their time has transpired, the Antioch church sends the two prophets back to Jerusalem with salutations of peace. Paul and Barnabas stay on in Antioch, teaching and preaching the Word of God along with many other local believers.[41]

Crisis in the Jewish Churches of Palestine

In Palestine, the dispersed Jewish believers are suffering persecution from unconverted Jews and Gentiles in their cities. They are particularly being oppressed by the affluent. The limited agricultural land cannot support a growing population. So those deprived of land are forced to become hired laborers. As a result, rich landowners are robbing some Christians of their land. Some are being hauled into court by wealthy men who scorn their faith.

At the same time, the influx of Hellenistic goods is causing a class of wealthy merchants to emerge. Consequently, some of the Christians are seeking opportunity to become wealthy as traders. Those in the church who are wealthy are being shown undue favoritism because the poor are afraid of offending them.

In addition, the Jewish Christians hear vague rumors about the council in Jerusalem. They hear that the Gentiles and the Jews have positioned themselves against the Law of Moses, under the influence of Paul of Tarsus.

They hear a very corrupted version of Paul's teaching. They are told that Paul is preaching that good works have nothing to do with salvation. Believing that this is now the position of the Twelve, some of the Jewish Christians begin to live loose and worldly lives. They are hurting one another with uncontrolled and critical speech, discriminating against the poor, and giving preferential treatment to the rich. Some of the worldly believers are ambitious to be teachers. There is also sickness in the churches. The crisis reaches the ears of James (the Lord's half-brother), and he is burdened to address it.[42]

JAMES WRITES THE LETTER OF JAMES

Year: A.D. 50

From: Jerusalem

To: The dispersed Jewish believers in Palestine

Provocation: James, the half-brother of Jesus, is often called "James the Righteous" or "James the Just," which implies his faithful observance to the Law. James encourages the Jewish believers in their time of trial and persecution. In reply to the false rumors that they have heard about Paul's teaching and the Jerusalem council, James distinguishes between the works of the Law and the works of faith. He makes clear that true faith will produce good works. (Paul makes this same point in Galatians, e.g. Galatians 5:6.) James reproves worldliness in the church. He admonishes those who are showing favoritism to the wealthy and rebukes the rich who are discriminating against the poor. James reproves critical speaking and exhorts the sick to ask for the elders to pray for their healing. The letter alludes to Jesus' "Sermon on the Mount" over twenty times. It also draws a lot from the Wisdom literature of the OT (namely, Proverbs).

Stop and read James

ENDNOTES

1. Mark 14:51—the reference to a "young man" is undoubtedly John Mark himself.

2. Acts 13:4-5.

3. The "column of the flagellation of St. Paul" remains in the city as a testimony to the beating of the two men.

4. Paul will experience this form of beating four more times over the next ten years (2 Corinthians 11:24).

5. Archaeological digs have uncovered the fact that the governor's daughter was also a believer. Further, tradition has it that at a later date Barnabas had a confrontation with Bar-Jesus in which he instigated the Jews to stone the apostle.

6. Sergius Paulus' family owned extensive property in Pisidian Antioch.

7. Acts 13:6-12.

8. From this point (Acts 13:13), Luke switches from writing "Barnabas and Saul" to "Paul and Barnabas," thus indicating that Paul took the lead.

9. Ten years later Paul will mention being involved in three shipwrecks and spending a night and a day in the open sea (2 Corinthians 11:25). Luke mentions nine sea voyages and only one shipwreck, which occurred after Paul penned 2 Corinthians. Adding up all of Paul's sea journeys, we discover that Paul traveled some 3,000 miles by sea.

10. Acts 13:13; 15:37-38.

11. Galatians 4:13-15.

12. Not to be confused with Antioch of Syria.

13. Acts 7.

14. Galatians 4:13-14.

15. Acts 13:14-52.

16. The Via Sebaste was built under Augustus in 6 B.C. It connected six military colonies, including Antioch of Pisidia.

17. Acts 14:1-7.

18. Like Pisidian Antioch, Lystra was made a Roman colony by Augustus in 25 B.C.

19. Hermes, whose Roman name is Mercury, was the clever messenger of the Greek gods. Zeus, whose Roman name is Jupiter, was the father of all the Greek gods as well as the humans.

20. The poet Ovid rehearses this tale.

21. 2 Corinthians 11:25.

22. 2 Timothy 3:10-11.

23. 2 Timothy 1:5.

24. Acts 16:1-3.

25. Galatians 6:17.

26. Acts 14:8-20.

27. Acts 20:4.

28. For a discussion on elders (also called overseers and presbyters), see my book *Rethinking the Wineskin*, Chapters 5 and 6.

29. Acts 14:20-23.

30. Acts 14:24-28.

31. The exact quote is "the Jews, who by the instigation of one Chrestus were evermore tumultuous, he banished from Rome."

32. Acts 18:1-2.

33. The mid-40s witnessed a revival of militancy among Judean free-dom-fighters. Tiberius Julius Alexander, procurator of Judea, crucified two of their leaders—Jacob and Simon, sons of the Judas who led the re-volt against the census in A.D. 6. These militants regarded any Jews who fraternized with the uncircumcised as traitors.

34. Galatians 2:11-13. Paul's rebuke to Peter is recorded in Galatians 2:14-21.

35. Galatians 5:10.

36. 2 Corinthians 12:7ff.

37. 2 Timothy 3:11.

38. 2 Corinthians 12:1-10. Paul refers to the thorn (splinter) as a "he" in the Greek... "a messenger of the adversary that he might buffet (harrass) me" (2 Corinthians 12:7, Young's Literal Translation & Wuest's New Testament Translation. See also Galations 5:10). In the Old Testa-ment, the "thorn in the flesh" was a metaphor to describe the enemies of God's people (Numbers 33:55). It seems that Paul's thorn was a Judaizer from Jerusalem who followed Paul's steps and sought to supplant the churches he had planted with slanderous rumors against Paul and his gospel.

39. This scenario is derived from mirror-reading Paul's words in Galatians. Mirror-reading is the process of reconstructing the historical situation of a NT letter by reading the author's response in the letter. The author's response "mirrors" the specific situation to which he is respond-ing. In the words of F.F. Bruce, when reading the NT letters "we are in a position of people listening to one end of a telephone conversation; we have to infer what is being said at the other end in order to reconstruct the situation for ourselves." (*Answers to Questions*, Grand Rapids: Zonder-van, 1972, p. 93).

40. Galatians 2:1.
41. Acts 15:1-35.
42. This scenario is derived from mirror-reading the letter of James.

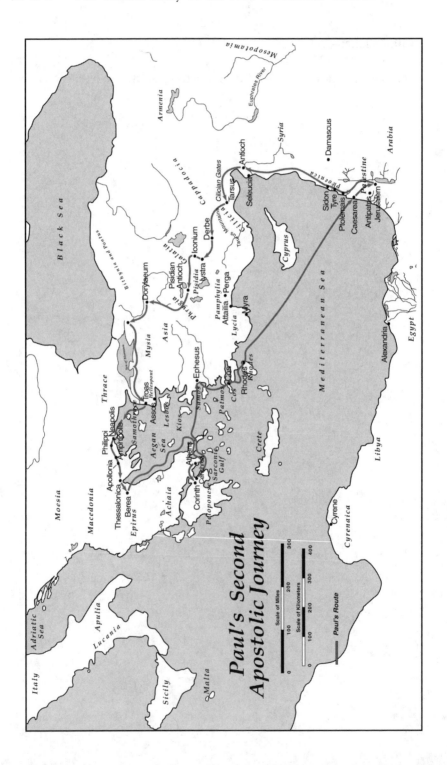

Paul's Second Apostolic Journey

CHAPTER 10

THE GRECIAN CHRONICLE

A.D. 50–A.D. 53

Then Paul chose Silas and departed, after being commended to the grace of the Lord by the brothers. He traveled through Syria and Cilicia, strengthening the churches (Acts 15:40-41).

PREVIEW OF PAUL'S SECOND APOSTOLIC JOURNEY

Time: 2 years
Years: A.D. 50–52
Miles Traveled: 2800 miles (1230 by sea; 1570 by land)
Churches Planted: (4) Philippi, Thessalonica, Berea, Corinth
Time Planted:
Philippi = 2-3 months
Thessalonica = 2-3 months
Berea = 1 month
Corinth = 18 months

Summer 50

Paul and Barnabas decide to revisit the churches in Galatia to check on their progress. However, the two men have a falling out over John Mark. Barnabas wishes to take him on the trip. Paul refuses, feeling that Mark deserted them on the first journey. The disagreement is so severe that Paul and Barnabas part ways.

Barnabas and Mark go to the Island of Cyprus (Barnabas' native land).[1] Paul takes Silas with him to South Galatia.[2] Silas has been a part of the Jerusalem church for 20 years, training under the Twelve.

Paul and Silas are approved and commended by the church to work together by God's grace. The two men set off on foot, first visiting and strengthening the churches in Cilicia and Syria.[3] They then make their way by land to the four churches in the hill countries of South Galatia. These churches have not seen Paul for about a year and a half.

The Galatian churches have survived their recent crisis! They received and embraced Paul's letter! Paul's gospel held and proved to be made of "gold, silver, and precious stone!"[4]

Timothy of Lystra

When the men come to Lystra, they take note of Timothy, a young man who shows signs of being called to the Lord's work. Timothy is respected by the believers in Lystra and Iconium. He probably withstood the Judaizers when they visited Galatia. (Timothy will later become a spiritual giant.)

Paul and Silas decide to take Timothy with them for the rest of their trip. The church of Lystra approves and Paul, along with the elders of the church, lays hands on Timothy. Spiritual gifts are imparted to Timothy and prophetic utterances are spoken over him.[5]

Since Timothy is a half-breed, he has never been circumcised.[6] Consequently, Paul circumcises Timothy so that he will not hinder the work. (The Jews in the region know that Timothy's father is a Greek. If Timothy is not circumcised, Paul will lose his link to the synagogue because the Jews will regard Timothy an apostate Jew. By circumcising Timothy, the Jews will give both Paul and Timothy a hearing.)

As the men pass through the towns of Syria, Cilicia, and Galatia,[7] they read the Jerusalem council letter to all the churches therein.[8] They also preach Christ with boldness in each church.[9] As a result, the churches are established in their faith and continue to increase in number.

Paul purposes to travel west into Asia, but the Holy Spirit forbids him from going. When the men come to the border of Mysia, they try to head north to Bithynia, but the Spirit again prevents them from going.[10]

A Visit to Troas

The men head northwest to a Roman colony called Troas. Troas is about 800 miles away from Antioch of Syria. Its population is about 30,000-40,000. In Troas, Paul receives a dream. In the dream, he sees a man from Macedonia beseeching him to come to Macedonia and supply help. The men interpret the dream to mean that God is calling them to preach the gospel in Macedonia.[11]

In the morning, the men head out to the Greek-speaking world of Macedonia and Achaia. (This area is modern Greece. Macedonia is Northern Greece. Achaia is Southern Greece.)

In Troas, Luke—a Gentile itinerant physician from Antioch, Syria—
joins Paul, Silas, and Timothy. Luke accompanies the men to Macedonia.[12]

A Church Planted in Philippi
Fall 50

From Troas, the men sail across the Aegean Sea and pass by a mountainous island called Samothrace which rises to 5,000 feet. The next day
they stop at Neapolis, the port city of Philippi. It only takes them two days
to sail from Troas to Neapolis for the weather is favorable. (It will take
Paul five days to sail the other direction, from Neapolis to Troas).[13]

The men take the great Roman road called the Via Egnatia (also
called the Egnatian Way). The Via Egnatia is a large, marble-covered military road that runs across the Balkan Peninsula, from the Aegean Sea to
the Adriatic. It is the most direct route between Rome and the East.[14]

The men come to the Roman colony of Philippi which is thirteen
miles inland from Neapolis.

Sharpening the Focus: Philippi is a Roman garrison town and the
chief city in the province of Macedonia. Unlike some of the other
Roman colonies that Paul visited, Philippi is thoroughly Roman-
ized. The chief language is Latin, though many speak Greek.
(Eighty percent of the inscriptions in Philippi are in Latin, com-
pared to forty percent which are in Pisidian Antioch.) The city is
governed by a proconsul (governor) whose headquarters is in Thessalonica. Therefore, the supreme authority to which a Philippian
can appeal is in another city.

Philippi is the famous battle site where Marc Antony defeat-
ed Octavian in 31 B.C. Octavian made the city a Roman colony,
settled some soldiers there, and gave the city the highest honor of
all—the *ius italicum* which made it an Italian city in every legal respect. In short, Philippi is a microcosm of Rome. There is no synagogue in Philippi. The Jewish population is too sparse. (Ten
Jewish men—called a *minyon*—are needed to establish a synagogue.) Instead, the Jews in the city maintain a *proseuche*, which is
a temporary place of prayer.

In Philippi, Paul, Silas, and Timothy meet a group of God-fearing
women who gather at a *proseuche* along the banks of the Gangites River.

Lydia, a lucrative purple merchant from Thyatira, is one of them.[15] Paul preaches Christ to the women, and God opens Lydia's heart. Lydia becomes the first convert in Europe. Lydia and her household are immediately baptized. She opens her home and insists that the men stay with her.

Day after day as the men walk to gather with the women by the riverside, a slave girl possessed with a pythonic spirit follows and mocks them aloud.[16] After many days pass, Paul's tolerance runs out. In the name of Jesus Christ, he casts out the Python spirit that has possessed the girl. Now delivered, the girl loses her powers of clairvoyance. This infuriates the men who own her, for they had been making a financial profit from her powers.

The owners drag Paul and Silas through the marketplace (also known as the *agora* in Greek and the *forum* in Latin) and bring them before the city magistrates (also called *praetors*). The owners accuse the men of disturbing the city and introducing illegal customs. They also make note that the two men are Jews.[17] Upon hearing the charges, the crowds are incited against Paul and Silas and join in the attack.

In a mad frenzy, the magistrates strip off their garments and hand Paul and Silas over to the *lictors* (the police attendants).[18] The two workers are beaten with birch rods without a trial.[19] The beating is severe. The men, shamed and humiliated by being beaten in public while naked, are left with open wounds in need of cleansing. Paul and Silas are thrown in jail, and a jailor is ordered to guard them securely. The two men are placed in the most secure cell in the prison, and their feet are placed in stocks, causing extreme discomfort.[20]

(The beating is illegal because Paul and Silas are Roman citizens. Roman citizens are exempt from scourging; they are exempt from arrest except in extreme cases; and they have the right to appeal to the emperor. Their cry of *Civis Romanus Sum*—I am a Roman citizen—was not heard amid the commotion that preceded their unjust beating.)

It is midnight. The prison where Paul and Silas are sitting is completely dark. With backs covered with bloody welts and legs stretched out in stocks, the two men pray and sing hymns to the Lord. The prisoners are all listening. Suddenly, an earthquake shakes the foundations of the jail, and the doors fling open. The men's stocks unloose also. The jailor awakes and sees the prison doors open. Immediately, he draws his sword to kill himself for he thinks the prisoners have escaped.[21]

Paul yells to the jailor that none of the prisoners have left. The jailor asks for a light to see the prisoners. He then falls down trembling before Paul and asks what he must do to be saved. Paul and Silas present Christ to the jailor and those in his home. The jailor bathes the wounds of the two men at a well in the prison courtyard. The jailor and his household are baptized and experience the joy of salvation. He then brings Paul and Silas to his home and feeds the men. Paul and Silas return to the prison.

At daybreak the next day, the magistrates release Paul and Silas and tell them to leave the city quietly. Paul, however, protests, saying that he and Silas are Roman citizens and it was illegal for them to have been beaten without a trial! To prove their Roman citizenship, Paul and Silas are probably carrying a *testatio*—a certified private copy of evidence of their birth and citizenship inscribed on the wax surface of a small wooden diptych (folding tablets).

The magistrates send word that Paul and Silas leave the city in secret. Paul returns word that he and Silas are Roman citizens and demands that they be escorted out of the city in public. He argues that because they were illegally shamed in public as criminals, they should be exonerated of the charges in public as well. Upon hearing that Paul and Silas are Roman citizens, the magistrates become fearful and comply with Paul's request. Paul and Silas are in no hurry to leave, however. They visit Lydia and encourage the believers. They then depart taking Timothy with them. But they leave Luke behind.

There is now a church in Philippi, mostly populated by God-fearing women. Two women named Euodia and Syntyche are in this church,[22] along with a man named Clement.[23] The Body of Jesus Christ—a community that expresses God's nature—is now present in Philippi!

A Church Planted in Thessalonica
A.D. 51

Paul, Silas, and Timothy head west on the Egnatian Way. After passing through the towns of Amphipolis (about 30 miles southwest of Philippi) and Apollonia, they come to the port city of Thessalonica. Thessalonica is about 90 miles southwest of Philippi.

Sharpening the Focus: Thessalonica is the capital of Macedonia and the largest city in Northern Greece. In fact, before Constantinople, Thessalonica was practically the capital of Greece, Illyricum, and Macedonia. Its population is around 200,000. It is a free Greek city, not a Roman colony. It mints its own coins and has its own form of government. Nevertheless, the city has close ties with Rome and the Emperor, and thus, is very sensitive to anything that would

> cause it to lose its "favored city" status. Thessalonica is also a center
> for communication and trade. It is an urban metropolitan city with
> a diverse population and many religions combining Greek, Roman,
> and Eastern ways of life and religions. Many Jews live here and
> share in the city's wealth. The women of Macedonia are noted for
> their independence.

Paul, Silas, and Timothy visit the Jewish synagogue on three consecutive Sabbaths. Paul preaches Christ from the OT Scriptures. Some of the Jews believe, including a large number of God-fearing Greeks and many of the leading women in the city. A Jew named Jason is converted and allows the apostolic workers to stay in his home.

Paul and Silas plant the church in Thessalonica, and it gathers in Jason's house. Paul presents to the young church a crucified and resurrected Christ. He instructs the Thessalonican converts to abandon their idols and to stop fornicating.[24] (Idolatry and fornication are a way of life in Greece.) Paul also speaks on the Kingdom of God to them, both its present and future dimensions. Paul labors with the church gently as a mother treats her children, yet sternly as a father admonishes them.[25]

Paul is out of money, so he begins mending tents to care for his needs. He works early in the morning and late in the evenings.[26] Paul pays his own way in everything, including his food. He does not want to be a burden on the Thessalonican believers while he is serving them with the gospel.[27] By his example, Paul teaches the church to work with its own hands. He also gives the believers the following standard: "If you don't work, you don't eat."[28] While Paul is laboring in Thessalonica, the church in Philippi graciously sends two financial gifts to help Paul and his companions.[29]

As the church in Thessalonica grows, the Jews become envious. They claim that Paul and Silas are preaching a king other than Caesar. In A.D. 16, Emperor Tiberius issued an imperial decree banning the prediction of a new king and kingdom in the cities of the empire. Paul is preaching the Kingdom of God, the coming return of Jesus, the worship of the one true God, and that the Gentiles should forsake their idols. All of these things make Paul an enemy of the State. Despite the opposition, Paul continues to proclaim the gospel and build the young church.[30] He warns the believers of the afflictions that they will suffer in the coming days and encourages them with stories about how the churches in Judea endured persecution.[31]

The opposition increases, and the Jews spread a rumor that Paul and Silas are criminals. (They no doubt heard about their imprisonment in Philippi.) The Jews stir up some local hoodlums to instigate a mob riot. The mob heads for Jason's house to search for Paul and Silas with the intention to bring them to the public assembly for trial. Paul and Silas are not there, however. So the mob drags Jason and some of the new converts to the civic assembly, accusing them of harboring men who are preaching a rival emperor!

The city rulers (also called *politarchs*) interrogate Jason. But they release him due to a lack of evidence of wrongdoing. Jason, however, must post bond. He is warned that if Paul and Silas do not leave the city, his property will be confiscated.

Accordingly, the brothers in Thessalonica send Paul and Silas secretly off under the cloak of darkness. But Paul leaves Timothy behind. A church—a community that expresses Jesus Christ—now exists in Thessalonica! The church in Thessalonica has three distinguished converts: Aristarchus, Secundus, and Demas.[32]

A Church Planted in Berea

Paul and Silas head 60 miles southwest on the Via Egnatia where they hit a resort-like town of cool mountains called Berea. Berea is rich and fertile. Farms are in abundance. The town is made up of older, high-class folk. Many Jewish merchants live there. Berea is a trading town and sports a high degree of literacy.

Timothy rejoins Paul and Silas. As is their custom, Paul and Silas go into the synagogue to preach Christ. The Bereans are open-minded Bible students. They eagerly hear and weigh Paul's message by the OT Scriptures. They express no hostility. In fact, many of the Bereans believe on Christ, including some upper-class Greek women. Sopater (also called Sosipater)[33] is one of the distinguished converts.[34]

What happens next is a repeat of Lystra. Jews from Thessalonica hear that Paul and Silas are in Berea, and they descend on the city and stir up the crowds against the two workers. Some of the Berean believers take Paul to the coast and send him off by sea to Athens in Achaia (Southern Greece). Silas and Timothy stay behind to encourage the newly founded Berean church. Paul sends word to Silas and Timothy to join him in Athens as soon as possible.[35] There is now a church in Berea—a community that expresses God's Son!

Rejection in Athens

Paul arrives in Athens alone. Athens is the cradle of Greek philosophy and democracy. It is a free Greek city with a population of no more than 50,000. Athens is full of idols and pagan temples—so much so that wherever Paul turns, statues, temples, and shrines fill his horizon. As Paul beholds the forest of pagan gods, his spirit is grieved. He takes curious note of one altar dedicated to the "Unknown God."

Timothy and Silas rejoin Paul. Paul tries to return to Thessalonica, but satan thwarts him.[36] He cannot get back into the city because the legal ban against him still remains. So Paul sends Timothy to Thessalonica to encourage the church and to find out how it is doing in its faith. He sends Silas to Philippi.[37]

Paul visits the synagogue in Athens and preaches Christ to the Jews and God-fearers. He also preaches Christ in the *agora*—the Athenian marketplace adorned with public buildings and colonnades. (The *agora* is the center of Athenian life and activity.)

Some of the Stoic and Epicurean philosophers engage Paul in debate. (Stoics believe that humans should be free from passion, so they suppress their affections and accept all things as the will of the gods. Epicureans believe that the chief aim of life is the pursuit of mental pleasure. They also believe that pain, suffering, and superstitions should be avoided.)

Some of the philosophers say that Paul is a babbler—a *spermologos* or seed-picker. This word refers to those who loaf about in the *agora* serving up sound bites of philosophy that they have picked up here and there. Others say that Paul declares a foreign god, for he preaches Jesus and the resurrection of the dead.[38]

The philosophers bring Paul to the Areopagus (also called Mars' Hill) to share his beliefs.[39] The Areopagus is the city council that decides on matters moral and religious. Paul is not brought there to stand trial. Rather, he is asked to deliver to the Athenians his "new" teaching. (The Athenians have a passion for anything "new" and making it the talk of the town. Consequently, they are eager to hear Paul's message.)

Tailoring his message to the Greek mind, Paul quotes some Greek poets.[40] He then explains who the "Unknown God" is. He preaches the Lord Jesus Christ. Yet when he begins speaking about a coming resurrection, some of the Athenians scoff at him. His teaching on the resurrection is foolishness to their ears.[41] Others, however, seek to hear Paul again on the matter.

There is little fruit in Athens, and no church is planted there. Only a handful of converts are made. Among them are Dionysius, a member of the Areopagus, a woman named Damaris, and some others.

A Church Planted in Corinth

Paul heads 40 miles west to the Roman colony of Corinth.[42] Because of his negative experiences in Greece thus far, he arrives in Corinth discouraged, dejected, and full of misgivings, or to put it in his own words, "in weakness, in fear, and in much trembling."[43]

Sharpening the Focus: Corinth is the capital of Achaia (Southern Greece). The city is named after the currant, a type of grape that grows in the region. Corinth is a large and prosperous city that is well becoming the largest and most prosperous city in Greece. Its population is estimated between 80,000 and 100,000. One third are slaves. The city is the major clearinghouse and slave market town for slaves being shipped westward from the East.

Being a Roman colony, the architecture in Corinth is Roman, and Latin is the official language. Corinth is a Roman city in a Greek setting. Religiously, the city is pluralistic and includes the Greek gods, especially Aphrodite and Apollos, as well as the imperial cult. It also includes a significant and long-standing Jewish community. There are many Jews in the city who have come from Rome due to Emperor Claudius' decree to expel all Jews from the Eternal City (Rome).

Corinth sits on a narrow isthmus of four and a half miles. The isthmus connects the western world with the eastern world. Thus you could hear a half dozen languages in the city in addition to the dominant Greek and Latin. Corinth is a great commercial center— a true melting pot. It caters to its many trafficking strangers in both food and entertainment. Consequently, Corinth's taverns are numerous and its prostitutes rampant. It is also a magnet for the socially ambitious. There are many opportunities for prosperity. So social climbing is a major occupation.

Corinth has a reputation for sexual immorality, luxury, self-promotion, and boasting. In fact, "Corinth" is a by-word for immorality. To act "Corinthian" or to "Corinthianize" is to engage in fornication. In fact, a prostitute is called a "Corinthian girl."

Corinth's wealth is generated by the manufacturing of Corinthian bronze and the Isthmian games. These games are the second largest sports event in the world next to the Olympics in Athens. These games are held twice a year in honor of Poseidon, god of the sea, and they are going on when Paul arrives (A.D. 51). The Isthmian crown, which Paul refers to as "a perishable crown" (1 Corinthians 9:25), is the principal reward presented at the games. Corinth is a very competitive city, being the first Greek city to have Roman gladiatorial contests.

Also prevalent in Corinth is one of the basic building blocks of Greco-Roman society. It is the patron-client relationship. Patrons are well-to-do individuals who become benefactors to less well-to-do folks (clients). The patron offers advice and protection to his client. In return, the client offers the patron various services, such as campaigning for him at elections, tending to his needs, and boosting the crowd at a family funeral. Stephanas, Phoebe, Lydia, and Philemon are some of the patrons that Paul will mention in the NT.

In this connection, while most of the converts in the churches that Paul plants are poor, a fair number of them are part of the urban elite (more on that later). This is partly because Paul's strategy is to plant churches in the most influential cities on the major trade routes of the Empire. Christianity is first and foremost an urban movement.

Soon after his arrival to Corinth, Paul meets Aquila (a native of Pontus, near the Black Sea) and his wife Priscilla (also called Prisca). Priscilla and Aquila are Jews who have been expelled from Rome by Emperor Claudius.[44] They, like Paul, are tentmakers. Because the Isthmian games are being held in Corinth at this time, there is a great need for temporary shelter. Thus the three tentmakers get plenty of business.

Crisis in Thessalonica

Silas and Timothy join Paul at Corinth. The church in Philippi has once again sent a financial gift to Paul, and Silas hands it to him. The money enables Paul to devote himself exclusively to the work of church planting.[45]

Timothy brings news from Thessalonica. The church is being persecuted, but it is standing steadfast for the Lord. It is also sounding forth the gospel. Believers from the churches in Macedonia (Philippi) and Achaia (Corinth) have visited the Thessalonican believers, and they are encouraged by their faith, their love, and their steadfastness in the midst of local persecution.

However, due to the pressure, some of the Thessalonican believers are returning back to their pagan lifestyles—namely fornication. Someone has died in the church recently, and the believers are grieving the loss. They also have questions about what happens to believers when they die. The church in Thessalonica has been on Paul's heart. He has desired to see the believers and has been lifting them up to the Lord day and night, asking for God to make a way for him to visit them.[46]

PAUL WRITES 1 THESSALONIANS

Year: A.D. 51

From: Corinth

To: The church in Thessalonica (which is about 6 months old)

Provocation: Paul encourages the church in the face of local persecution and revisits some of what he said to them when planting the church. He brings comfort to the church about the person who has passed away. The letter also anticipates a visit from the Judaizers. Paul, therefore, responds to the common accusations against him before those accusations are made. (The smear campaign against Paul includes accusations that he uses flattery and distortions of the truth to gain converts, and he is motivated by greed.) At the end of the letter, he reminds the believers about the soon coming Day of the Lord's wrath. Paul closes by exhorting the church to take care of one another and to appreciate and esteem those individuals (himself, Silas, and Timothy) who labor among them. The letter is sent by the hand of Timothy and Silas.

Stop and read 1 Thessalonians

Paul goes into the Corinthian synagogue every Sabbath and preaches Christ persuasively to both Jews and Gentiles.[47] As Paul continues to preach in the synagogue, the Jews oppose and revile him. So he leaves the synagogue, shaking out the dust from his clothes saying to them, "Your blood be upon your own heads. I am clear of it. From now on I will go to the Gentiles."

Paul leads Stephanas and his household to the Lord. They are the first converts in the city.[48] Erastus, the city treasurer,[49] and Quartus are also converted. A Roman citizen named Gaius Titius Justus is brought to Christ as well. Gaius is a well-to-do God-fearer with a large home that is located next door to the synagogue. The home holds about 50-60 people. Gaius opens up his home for Paul to minister in and for the believers to gather.[50]

Crispus (the synagogue ruler) and his household are also converted and baptized along with some others. (Paul only baptizes Crispus, Gaius, and the household of Stephanas. They, along with Priscilla and Aquila, baptize the other converts.)[51]

As is his custom when he plants a church, Paul grounds the Corinthians on nothing but Christ and His cross.[52] He declares to them that they are called into the fellowship of God's Son, and he brings them into that very experience.[53] He also tells them stories of the perseverance of other churches, including the church in Thessalonica.[54]

The Body of Jesus Christ is now present in Corinth, expressing God's nature in the city. While a number of the believers are of high standing, most are uneducated and poor.[55] (This is true for all the churches that Paul plants.)

The Lord appears to Paul in a vision and encourages him to not be afraid, but to speak boldly. The Lord promises Paul that no one will harm him while he is laboring in Corinth and that He (Christ) has many people in the city. Consequently, Paul stays in Corinth for a total of eighteen months, planting the church and evangelizing the city. As a token of thanksgiving to God for His promise of protection, Paul lets his hair grow long as part of a voluntary Nazarite vow.[56]

Spring 52

While Paul is laboring in Corinth, he gets word that the Thessalonican believers misunderstood what he wrote about the Lord's second coming in his first letter. The church mistakenly believes that the Day of the Lord's wrath is at hand. As a result, many are disturbed in spirit. Some quit their jobs in anticipation of the Lord's coming and are living off the other believers who work for a living. Having too much time on their hands, these individuals are acting as "busybodies" in the lives of others.[57]

PAUL WRITES 2 THESSALONIANS

Year: A.D. 52

From: Corinth

To: The church in Thessalonica (which is about 10 months old)

Provocation: Paul comforts the church in its affliction and assures the believers that God will bring vengeance on those who do the afflicting. He corrects their misunderstanding about the Day of the Lord and Christ's return, and clarifies what he taught concerning it when he was first with them. He ends the letter by correcting those brothers who have quit their jobs and instructs the church to not associate with them as long as they are living undisciplined lives. Paul ends by encouraging the whole church to not become weary in well-doing.

Stop and read 2 Thessalonians

The money that Silas brought to Paul from Philippi has run out. So Paul resumes his work as a tentmaker along with Priscilla and Aquila. Paul refuses to take money from the Corinthian believers, lest he be a burden on them. He stands by his conviction to offer his gospel free of charge.[58]

Summer 53

The Jews in Corinth attack Paul and bring him before the local tribunal. They accuse Paul of propagating an illegal religion. The Jews argue that the message that Paul is preaching is not Judaism, which is protected under Roman law. As Paul is about to defend himself, Lucius Junius Gallio, the governor (or proconsul) of Southern Greece, stops the proceedings. He refuses to take up the case because he deems it to be an internal dispute among the Jewish community regarding differences of religious interpretation. Gallio drives everyone from his tribunal.[59]

Immediately, some Greek bystanders seize Sosthenes, the new synagogue ruler, and beat him in front of the tribunal. Gallio turns a blind eye to the anti-Jewish sentiment.

After spending some more time in Corinth, Paul leaves and sets sail across the Aegean Sea to the city of Ephesus. He takes Priscilla and Aquila with him. On their way, they stop at a little town seven miles east of Corinth called Cenchrea. Cenchrea is the seaport of Corinth. Before sailing to Ephesus, Paul cuts his hair and ends his temporary Nazarite vow.[60]

Paul, Priscilla, and Aquila set sail to the city of Ephesus in Asia Minor. Priscilla and Aquila settle there and set up their tentmaking business. Paul goes to the synagogue briefly and preaches to the Jews. The Jews ask him to stay longer, but he cannot. He tells them that he plans to return, God willing.

Paul sails to Caesarea and from there he visits the church in Jerusalem. He greets the Jerusalem church and returns to his home base in Antioch of Syria where he rests. Silas heads back to Jerusalem and Timothy returns to Lystra.[61]

ENDNOTES

1. According to tradition, Barnabas was martyred in the city of Salamis in Cyprus and was secretly buried by Mark.

2. Acts 15:36-40.

3. Acts 15:41.

4. A metaphor that Paul uses in 1 Corinthians 3:10-12 for a work that is built with God's life rather than with man's strength.

5. 1 Timothy 1:18; 4:14; 2 Timothy 1:6.

6. Timothy's father is Greek, and his mother is Jewish.

7. Luke uses the term "Phrygia and Galatia" in Acts 16:6, but he is referring to Phrygian Galatia (Phrygia Galatica) as opposed to Asian Galatia. In general, Luke mostly uses ethnic and regional designations while Paul in his epistles uses provincial designations.

8. Acts 16:1ff.

9. Acts 16:3 in the Western Text. The Western Text represents a family of early manuscripts of the NT characterized by longer readings than those found in other families of the NT text.

10. Acts 16:6-8.

11. It is highly likely that the man Paul saw in the dream was Luke. But Luke did not wish to identify the man so as not to draw attention to himself (as is the case throughout Acts).

12. Acts 16:8-11; Colossians 4:14.

13. Acts 20:6.

14. Philippi, Amphipolis, Apollonia, and Thessalonica all stand on the Egnatian Way.

15. That Lydia had a house and servants ("household") makes her a woman of some means and of some social significance. Further, that her trade dealt with royal purple confirms this as well. Dealing in royal purple (the murdex dye) was an imperial monopoly. Those who traded it were typically members of Caesar's household.

16. A Python spirit is a demon inspired by Apollo, the Python deity often consulted through the oracle at Delphi.

17. Since the Jews have recently been expelled from Rome, and Philippi is a Roman colony, Paul and Silas are viewed with disfavor simply because they are Jews.

18. The *lictors* ("rod bearers") carried bundles of rods (called *fasces*) as a sign of their office.

19. 1 Thessalonians 2:2. This is the second time Paul is beaten with rods. He will be beaten one more time over the next six years (2 Corinthians 11:25).

20. The prisoner in stocks must sleep on his side or in a sitting position. Changing positions to avoid cramping is nearly impossible. The discomfort of a prisoner can turn to excruciating pain simply by increasing the distance between the left and right foot.

21. Allowing prisoners to escape is a capital offense.

22. Acts 16:12-40; Philippians 4:2.

23. Philippians 4:3.

24. 1 Thessalonians 1:9; 4:2ff.

25. 1 Thessalonians 2:7-11.

26. 1 Thessalonians 2:9.

27. 2 Thessalonians 3:8.

28. 1 Thessalonians 4:11; 2 Thessalonians 3:10.

29. Philippians 4:15-16.

30. 1 Thessalonians 1:6; 2:2.

31. 1 Thessalonians 3:4; 2:14.

32. Acts 17:1-9; Acts 20:4; 2 Timothy 4:10.

33. In his letters, Paul refers to people by their formal names while Luke refers to them by their familiar names. Paul says Sosipater while Luke says Sopater. Paul speaks of Prisca while Luke calls her Priscilla, etc.

34. Acts 20:4; Romans 16:21.

35. Acts 17:10-15.

36. Acts 17:16-34; 1 Thessalonians 2:18.

37. This scenario is derived from piecing together Acts 17:15, 18:5, and 1 Thessalonians 3:1-5.

38. The Greeks believe in the immortality of the soul, but not the resurrection of the body.

39. During this period, the Areopagus was an aristocratic body composed of the local elite. Areopagus means "the hill of Ares." The Areopagus in Athens took its name from the Greek god of war, Ares, whose Roman name is Mars. The hill of Ares was the original meeting place for the Areopagus. During Paul's day, except for investigating cases of homicide, the council met in the Royal Porch in the Athenian marketplace.

40. In Acts 17:28, Paul quotes Epimenides the Cretan (c. 600 B.C.) and Aratus the Cilician (b. 310 B.C.) respectively. (Paul was very conversant with Greco-Roman philosophy and poetry. In 1 Corinthians 15:33, he quotes Menander, the author of the Greek comedy Thais.)

41. 1 Corinthians 1:17-23.

42. Paul probably sailed from Piraeus between the islands of Salamis and Aegina to the harbor of Cenchrea on the eastern shore of the Isthmus of Corinth. It probably took Paul two or three hours to walk from Cenchrea to Corinth.

43. 1 Corinthians 2:3.

44. Some scholars believe that Priscilla was Roman and belonged to the Roman family called *gens Prisca*. If this is true, it would explain why both Luke and Paul always put her name before her husband's. It is because of her higher social class.

45. 2 Corinthians 11:9; Philippians 4:14-16.

46. This scenario is derived from mirror-reading Paul's words in 1 Thessalonians.

47. Acts 18:1ff.

48. 1 Corinthians 16:15.

49. Or director of public works. Erastus is a freedman (a former slave).

50. Gaius and Titius Justus are the same person (Acts 18:7; 1 Corinthians 1:14; Romans 16:23— written from Corinth).

51. 1 Corinthians 1:14-17.

52. 1 Corinthians 2:1-2.

53. 1 Corinthians 1:9.

54. 2 Thessalonians 1:4.

55. 1 Corinthians 1:26-27. W.M. Ramsey wrote that Christianity "spread first among the educated more rapidly than among the uneducated." Lydia in Philippi, many of "the leading women" of Thessalonica, Dionysius of Athens, Erastus, Stephanus, Crispus, Gaius Titius Justus, and Sosthenes (who will become a Christian shortly) of Corinth all belong to the higher social strata of Greece.

56. Numbers 6:1ff.

57. This scenario is derived from mirror-reading Paul's words in 2 Thessalonians.

58. 1 Corinthians 9; 2 Corinthians 11:7-9; 12:13-18.

59. Gallio was the older brother of Annaeus Seneca, the famous Stoic philosopher and playwright who tutored Emperor Nero.

60. This was not a formal Nazarite vow, which could not have been properly undertaken outside the Holy Land. It was rather a private vow of thanksgiving.

61. We assume that Silas and Timothy returned to their hometowns.

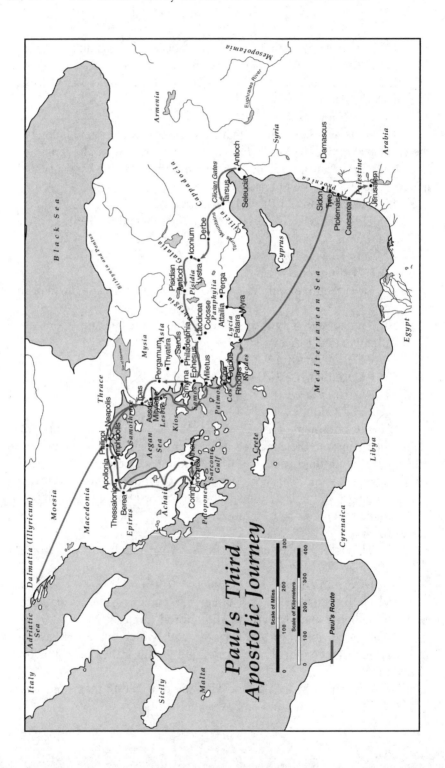

Paul's Third Apostolic Journey

CHAPTER 11

THE EPHESIAN CHRONICLE

A.D. 54–A.D. 58

While Apollos was in Corinth, Paul traveled through the interior regions and came to Ephesus. He found some disciples (Acts 19:1).

PREVIEW OF PAUL'S THIRD APOSTOLIC JOURNEY

Time: 3 years

Years: A.D. 54–57

Miles Traveled: 1375 miles

Churches Planted: (11+) Paul planted the church in Ephesus. Epaphras planted the churches in Laodicea, Colosse, and Hierapolis. Paul's other coworkers planted churches throughout Asia Minor. Among them are Smyrna, Thyatira, Sardis, Philadelphia, and Pergamum. Paul planted churches in Troas and Illyricum (Dalmatia).

Time planted:

Ephesus = 3 years

The others churches in Asia Minor = Unknown

Troas = Unknown

Illyricum (Dalmatia) = Unknown

Rome (Transplanted) = Unknown

Spring 54

While in Antioch, Syria, Paul plots three things. They will set the course for the rest of his ministry until his death:

- He decides to begin the Jerusalem relief fund. This is a collection campaign taken from among all of the Gentile churches that Paul planted to relieve the chronic poverty of the Jerusalem Christians. Paul does this to mend the rift between the Hebrew and Gentile believers. He sends a letter to the churches in Galatia, telling them about the relief fund and gives them specific instructions on how to begin collecting for it.[1]

- Paul is approximately 50 years old. He is an old man according to first-century standards. So he decides to train apostolic workers in Ephesus in the same way that Jesus Christ trained the twelve apostles in Galilee. The men Paul trains are Gentiles and will represent the Gentile churches when they deliver the relief fund to Jerusalem.[2]
- Paul has a desire to take the gospel to Rome and then to Spain. He plans to accomplish this on his fourth journey, after he plants the church in Ephesus and brings the relief fund to Jerusalem.[3]

Apollos

In Ephesus, Priscilla and Aquila begin visiting the synagogue to locate any Jewish or God-fearing seekers. They follow up with those who were impressed with Paul's message when he was there. Priscilla and Aquila share the gospel with a man named Epaenetus, and he receives it. Epaenetus becomes the first convert in Ephesus.[4]

A cultured, Grecian (Hellenistic) Jew named Apollos comes to Ephesus. Apollos is from Alexandria, Egypt.[5] First-century Alexandria is a metropolis. It is the second largest city in the Empire with a population of about one million. It contains a huge ghetto of Jews.

Apollos is an educated man and knows the OT Scriptures well. He is an impressive orator who is extremely eloquent and charismatic.[6] Apollos is a believer, but there is a gap in his knowledge of the Lord.[7] He preaches Christ in the synagogue with the glow of the Spirit, explaining the story of Jesus.[8] But he knows nothing about Christian baptism. He only knows the baptism of John the Baptist.

Priscilla and Aquila hear him preach and invite him to their home. The couple instructs Apollos more accurately in the gospel. Some of the believers from Corinth are in Ephesus visiting Priscilla and Aquila. Upon meeting Apollos, they invite him to visit the church in Corinth.[9] Apollos wishes to go, and Priscilla and Aquila write Corinth a letter of commendation for

Apollos, asking them to receive him. Apollos leaves Ephesus for Corinth with the letter.

Corinth Has Visitors
Summer 54

When Apollos arrives in Corinth, he argues with and refutes the local Jews in the synagogue with his apologetic savvy, his logic, and his rhetoric. He also encourages the Corinthian believers who have believed by grace.

The Corinthians are spellbound by Apollos' masterful Greco-Roman oratory. As a result, some of the Corinthian believers, mostly made up of Greeks, begin to rally around Apollos. Because Apollos is so gifted a speaker, they begin to criticize Paul as a less capable orator and a less spiritual person.[10] (The Greeks are known for equating knowledge and great oratory with spirituality.)[11]

When Apollos leaves, Barnabas pays a visit to Corinth to strengthen the church.[12] Peter and his wife also visit Corinth.[13] Peter is noted for his signs and wonders. As is his custom when visiting a church, Peter performs some healings in the city. As a consequence, a Corinthian party, mostly made up of Jews, develops around Peter.[14] (The Jews are known for being awed by signs and wonders.)[15]

In reaction to the growing divisions, some of the Corinthians declare that Paul is their only apostle, while others are claiming that they exclusively follow Christ and not men. The church in Corinth is becoming fractured. Parties are developing around the different apostolic workers who have visited the church.[16]

Paul leaves Antioch with Titus. The two men head up through Tarsus through the Cilician Gates to South Galatia. They visit and encourage all the Galatian churches, strengthening them in their faith. The Galatian churches have not seen Paul in four years!

Paul gives each church instructions concerning the Jerusalem relief fund. From South Galatia, Paul picks up Gaius (from Derbe) and Timothy (from Lystra) to accompany him to Ephesus.

A New Work in Ephesus

Paul, Titus, Gaius, and Timothy take the upper country and make their way by land to Ephesus in Asia Minor. When they come to Ephesus, they meet three brothers whom Paul has sent for: Sopater (of Berea),[17] Aristarchus,[18] and Secundus (both of Thessalonica). Paul will train these six men in Ephesus for the work of planting churches. Their mission is to expand the community that God has purposed from the beginning so that His nature will be expressed throughout the earth. These men will also serve as delegates from their respective churches when delivering the relief fund to the church in Jerusalem.[19]

All six men have experienced the life of the church for at least three years, and they are going to be trained to be apostolic workers under the tutelage of Paul.[20] These men are:

- Titus from Antioch
- Timothy from Lystra
- Gaius from Derbe
- Sopater from Berea
- Aristarchus from Thessalonica
- Secundus from Thessalonica

Sharpening the Focus: Ephesus is a free Greek city located at the mouth of the Cayster River, which flows into the Aegean Sea. It is the largest city in Asia Minor. The population of Ephesus is 225,000, and it has a large Jewish population.

Ephesus is a seaport and is the first ranking city of Asia Minor in commerce, wealth, politics, and religion. It is the New York of the ancient world. The city has a central hub that connects the eastern world with the western world, making it a magnificent city of wealth. For this reason, the historian Pliny called it "the ornament of Asia" and "the vanity fair of Asia." It is the communications hub for virtually every part of Asia. The emperor's college of messengers is also based in the city.

The city's wealth is reflected everywhere, from its marble-paved main street to the mosaic floors in its aristocratic homes. One of the seven wonders of the world is also there: the great temple of Artemis (in Latin her name is Diana; she is a nature-fertility goddess). It took 220 years to build this temple. Built out of pure white marble, it is the largest building in existence at this time and is known worldwide. The temple is 220 feet by 425 feet. It is supported by 127 columns, each of them 60 feet high, and is adorned by some of the greatest sculptors of the age. In the temple resides a statue of Diana, which the Ephesians believe fell from the sky. Ephesus is also the center for magical arts and occult practices in Asia.

A Church Planted in Ephesus

When Paul arrives in Ephesus, he meets twelve disciples of John the Baptist. Paul leads them all to Christ and baptizes them in the name of Jesus. He then lays his hands on them, and the Holy Spirit falls on each one. The twelve men begin to speak in tongues and prophesy.

These twelve men, along with Priscilla, Aquila, and Epaenetus, form the nucleus of the Ephesian church. Two other Greek converts are made and are added to the church. In time, they will be added to the six Gentiles that Paul is training to be apostolic workers, thus making a total of eight. The two Greek converts are:

- Tychicus
- Trophimus

There is a community in the great city of Ephesus who is expressing God's divine nature—the Body of Christ is born in Asia!

The Hall of Tyrannus

For three months, Paul preaches Christ with great power in the Ephesian synagogue. The Jews reject and malign his message, so Paul moves his ministry center to the Hall of Tyrannus—a lecture hall that he rents. Every day from 11 a.m. to 4 p.m., Paul preaches Christ, trains the eight apprentices that are with him, and lays a foundation for the Ephesian church.[21] (Tyrannus probably lectured in the morning, while Paul used the hall in the afternoon. In the Greco-Roman world, the business day ended at 11 a.m. when most of the city ate a meal followed by a siesta.)[22]

Paul mends tents in the morning, beginning before sunrise, preaches in the afternoon, then mends tents again in the evening. With his own hands, Paul supports himself and the eight men he is training. He often goes hungry and thirsty.[23]

The community of Christians in Ephesus is meeting from house to house while Paul conducts the work from the Hall of Tyrannus. One of the homes where the church gathers is the house of Priscilla and Aquila.[24] Paul has received a wide-open door to preach the gospel in Ephesus; however, he encounters many adversaries.[25] On top of this, on a daily basis he experiences anxiety over the well-being of the eight churches he has planted.[26]

Paul will preach and teach in the Hall of Tyrannus for two years. During that time, he will unfold the "whole will and purpose of God."[27] He will also counsel the believers on a regular basis, admonishing them with tears.[28] Many people from Asia, both Jews and Greeks, will visit the new work in Ephesus and hear Paul preach. One such man is Philemon, a well-to-do business man from the wealthy town of Colosse (about 100 miles east of Ephesus).

Philemon owns a slave named Onesimus. Paul leads Philemon to Christ, and he becomes a help to Paul. After their short stay, Philemon and Onesimus head back to their home in Colosse.

Around the same time, a man named Epaphras visits Ephesus. Epaphras is also from Colosse. Paul leads him to the Lord, and Epaphras stays in Ephesus for a time to learn from Paul and the church. Epaphras then heads back to Colosse.

At the end of two years, Paul will send his eight apprentice-companions throughout the region. These men will plant new churches all over Asia Minor. Some of these churches are listed in Revelation chapters 2 and 3. As a result of Paul's ministry in Ephesus and his sending out of these men to the neighboring cities, "the whole of Asia Minor" will hear the word of the Lord.[29] The Body of Jesus Christ—the community who expresses God's nature—is growing in Ephesus as well as throughout all of Asia Minor. Paul will spend a total of three years laboring in Ephesus. This is his longest church planting visit.[30]

October 13, 54

Emperor Claudius dies. His wife Agrippina poisons him with his favorite dish—mushrooms—so that her son, Nero, can become emperor. Nero's first five years as emperor will be relatively moderate. But his pretense of morality and fairness will begin to run out in A.D. 59 when he has his mother killed.[31]

Power Encounters in Ephesus

While in Ephesus, Paul performs extraordinary miracles. Sweat-rags and aprons that have had contact with his body are taken from him and used to heal the sick and cast out demons. As a result, a great number of magicians are converted. They burn their magical scrolls and dispel their secrets in public. The value of all the documents that go up in smoke amounts to 50,000 drachmas.[32] Among the books burned are the so-called "Ephesian letters" which are charms believed to make the bearers irresistible.

Upon seeing the miracles that Paul works by invoking the name of Jesus, some itinerant (traveling) Jewish exorcists try to cast out demons using the Lord's name. Seven sons of a Jewish chief priest named Sceva attempt to do this. When they try to use the name of Jesus in casting out a devil from someone, the evil spirit says to them, "Jesus I know, and Paul I know, but who are you?"

The demon-possessed man brutally beats the sons of Sceva. The news of this incident spreads throughout the city and the people are filled with awe. The name of Jesus is magnified and shown to be something that cannot be trifled with lightly.[33]

Crisis in Corinth

Apollos returns to Ephesus from his visit to Corinth. He brings Sosthenes with him, the former ruler of the synagogue. Sosthenes has since become a Christian.[34] Apollos meets with Paul and informs him about the problems the church is having. Apollos tells Paul that some in the Corinthian church are reverting back to their heathen lifestyles. They are committing fornication, worshipping idols, and stealing from one another.[35]

PAUL WRITES CORINTHIANS A

(This letter is lost to us.)

Year: A.D. 54

From: Ephesus

To: The church in Corinth (which is 4 years old)

Provocation: Provoked by Apollos' report, Paul urges the Corinthians to no longer keep company with fornicators, idolaters, and thieves in the church. He also explains to them his desire to have a Jerusalem relief fund. Finally, Paul tells the Corinthians that he will visit them after he leaves Ephesus. He will then visit the churches in Macedonia and return again to Corinth, after which he will take the relief fund to Jerusalem in Judea (see 2 Corinthians 1:15-16).

Paul sends the letter with Titus. While in Corinth, Titus helps the Corinthian believers to begin collecting money for the Jerusalem relief fund.[36] Titus leaves and returns to Ephesus.

The doctrine of Hellenistic dualism begins to gain ground in Corinth. According to this doctrine, if individuals have the Spirit of God, they live above the earthly plane and are unaffected by what they do with their bodies. The material world is temporary so it does not matter what kind of physical behavior in which a person engages. Thus sexual immorality is acceptable. Further, since God is not interested in the physical world, there will be no resurrection of the dead.

Spring 55

Some Corinthian Christians who work for a business woman named Chloe pay a visit to Ephesus. Chloe's people fill Paul's ears with the horrors of the Corinthian church. They tell him the following:

- There is division, jealousy, and strife among the believers. The church is fracturing into four parties. Some of the Greeks are showing exclusive loyalty to Apollos, saying "I follow Apollos." They equate his Greek oratory style with "higher" wisdom and knowledge. Some of the Jews are showing exclusive loyalty to Peter, saying "I follow Peter." They are chasing after signs and wonders. Still others are making the elitist claim that they exclusively follow Christ and have no need of any apostle. "I follow Christ" is their motto. Finally, there are some who are boasting exclusive loyalty to Paul, pitting him in competition with the other workers saying, "I follow Paul."

Paul is disturbed by hearing this news, so he begins addressing the problems in a letter. When Paul finishes the letter, he is visited by three respected brothers from the church in Corinth—Stephanas, Fortunatus, and Achaicus. The three men singe Paul's ears with more disturbing news about the Corinthian assembly.[37] They report to him the following:

- A brother in the church is committing incest and the believers are ignoring it. Some are even boasting in their Christian liberty while this is going on.
- Some of the brothers are taking one another to court.
- Some of the brothers who have been influenced by Hellenistic dualism are visiting prostitutes and engaging in gluttony, thinking that what they do with their bodies has no bearing on their spirits. Their slogans are "everything is permissible (lawful) for me" and "food for the stomach and the stomach for food."
- A number of the believers are very sick. A few of them have died recently.
- The slaves work late and cannot make the church meetings on time. The well-to-do are not waiting for them, but are eating the Lord's Supper ahead of their poor brethren.[38] Still worse, the well-to-do are treating the Lord's Supper as if it were a private dinner party. They are

gorging themselves on the food and getting drunk on the wine.[39]

- There is quarreling over the issue of the marriage veil. Some of the wives are removing their marriage veils when they pray and prophesy in the church meetings. This has caused some who have visited them to accuse the wives of being immoral.[40] Their husbands have asked them to wear the veil in the meetings, but the women are contentiously arguing that they are at liberty to do as they wish.

Stephanas, Fortunatus, and Achaicus also hand Paul a letter from the church that is packed with questions. Here are some of the questions contained in that letter:

- Didn't you tell us not to associate with sexually immoral people in the world? How can we do that since most of the people we work with engage in sexual immorality?
- Some in the church who read your last letter about abstaining from sexual immorality are practicing sexual abstinence in their marriages. They have a saying among them which is: "It is not good for a man to touch a woman." Do you agree with this?
- Some of the believers have unsaved spouses. Should they divorce them or stay married?
- Some of the brothers who are betrothed (engaged) to women in the church are not sure if they should pursue marriage. What is your opinion?
- Is it wrong to buy meat that has been offered to idols at the pagan meat markets? Some are arguing that idols are just human sculptures and the gods that they represent do not exist. They believe it does not matter if one eats meat offered to idols. Others disagree with this position and feel eating such meat is sinful.
- Is it wrong to dine in pagan temples?[41] Some believe this is a social necessity and pagan gods do not exist anyway, so how could it be wrong? Others believe that the consecration to idols does something to the meat so they cannot eat with a clear conscience.
- Some are critical of you, Paul, and are raising questions about the genuineness of your apostolic calling. They are

asking why you do not take money as the other apostles do, like Peter and Apollos.[42]

- The meetings of the church are chaotic. The gift of tongues is exalted by some because it is the language of the angels. Many are speaking in tongues at the same time during the meetings, and it is creating massive confusion. Further, some of the married women are challenging those who are prophesying with many questions. This is creating both confusion and disruption in our gatherings. What should we do about this?

- Some in the church who have been influenced by Hellenistic dualism are denying a future resurrection. Can you address this?

- Please go over your instructions concerning the Jerusalem relief fund. There is some confusion over it.

Paul responds to what he has heard from Stephanas, Fortunatus, and Achaicus immediately, expanding the letter he had written after hearing the report from Chloe's people.[43] We will call this letter CORINTHIANS B. This is our 1 Corinthians. Paul asks Apollos to visit the church in Corinth with some others, but it turns out not to be the Lord's will for Apollos to visit at this time. Timothy is not with Paul as he pens the letter. But Paul plans to send him to Corinth when he returns. He wants Timothy to encourage the church as well as to see how it receives the letter.

PAUL WRITES CORINTHIANS B
(This is our 1 Corinthians.)

Year: Spring 55
From: Ephesus
To: The church in Corinth (which is about 5 years old)
Provocation: In chapters 1-4, Paul addresses the report that he has heard from Chloe's people. In chapters 5-6, Paul addresses the issues of sexual immorality and civil litigation. In chapters 7-15, he answers the church's list of questions. In chapter 16, Paul goes over his instructions for collecting the Jerusalem relief fund. He then gives the church his new travel plans, which had changed from before. Instead of traveling from Ephesus to Corinth, then to Macedonia,

and then back to Corinth as he first planned, he will travel from Ephesus to Macedonia and then make one long visit to Corinth. Paul closes the letter by commending Timothy, who will visit them shortly, and exhorting the church to yield to Stephanas and other workers during their present crisis. He ends by sending greetings from the churches in Asia Minor, Priscilla, Aquila, the church in Ephesus (that meets in Priscilla and Aquila's house), and the brothers whom Paul is training.

Stop and read 1 Corinthians

The letter is sent to Corinth by the hand of Stephanas, Fortunatus, and Achaicus. Timothy sees Paul, and Paul sends him to Corinth.

A Church Transplanted in Rome

Nero lifts the ban on the Jews and allows them to return to Rome. When Paul gets wind of this, he sends Priscilla and Aquila back to Rome. The couple find a home in the Aventine district, a very nice part of the city. Paul wants to have a Gentile church in the Eternal City, and he wants it started before the Jews trickle back in.

Consequently, Paul sends word to the Gentile churches and asks some of the believers in each church to pick up and move to the unhappy city of Rome. He also asks a few of his Jewish relatives from Jerusalem to move there.[44]

In effect, Paul transplants a number of his Gentile converts in Rome, along with some Jewish believers, thus creating a cosmopolitan church to match the cosmopolitan capital. Some of the people whom Paul sends to Rome are:[45]

- Priscilla from Ephesus
- Aquila from Ephesus
- Epaenetus from Ephesus
- Phoebe from Cenchrea
- Rufus from Syrian Antioch
- Andronicus from Jerusalem[46]
- Junias from Jerusalem
- Urbanus from Macedonia
- Apelles from Asia Minor

Sharpening the Focus: First-century Rome is a cosmopolitan city—the melting pot of the entire world. It is the Roman Empire in microcosm with representatives of every race, ethnic group, social status, and religion. The city is a perfect square—about two and one-half miles by two and one-half miles (many of the poor are densely populated outside the city walls). Rome sits on seven hills and contains fourteen districts. The city has 1,790 palaces and 46,602 tenement apartments (called *insulas*).

The population is about one million. Citizens range from the miserably poor to the lavishly rich. Half the population is made up of slaves, making it the "slave capital of the world." Many of the freedmen live in horrible poverty. The Roman poet Juvenal (A.D. 110) described Rome as a filthy sewer into which flowed every abominable dreg. The Stoic philosopher Seneca (A.D. 55) spoke of Rome as a cesspool of iniquity.

The Jewish population is large and free, sitting around 40,000-60,000. Jews are spread all over the city, but most of them live in a pocket of the city called the Trastevere area. Rome has about a dozen synagogues.

All but the rich (excluding the homeless) live in *insulas*. Most *insulas* are seven stories high, covering an entire block. Heat and light are very inadequate. The first floor is used for shops. The second floor is very expensive. The poor live on the third floor or above. The third-floor rooms are very tiny. They do not have running water. They are also poorly built and sometimes collapse, killing the tenants inside. The *insulas* are made mostly of timber, so they are a fire hazard in the dry season.

The city is extremely crowded with densely packed apartments. It is also unbearably noisy. From dawn to dusk, there is constant babbling in the streets and from the apartments. It is hard to sleep because of the racket. There is no public transportation and no street lighting (these things will not appear in Rome until the fourth century).

While the main concourses of the city are attractive, the back streets are dirty, unlighted, pitiful, and smelly. They are littered with garbage and covered with flies. The garbage is never removed. The residents must await a heavy downpour to flush it into the

Tiber River. In the pits along the sideways you can see the bodies of the poor who could not afford burials. If you are poor, Rome is the worst place to live on planet Earth.

Those whom Paul asked to move to Rome relocate. The Body of Jesus Christ has come to Rome! A community who reflects the community of the Godhead is born in the Eternal City!

An Urgent Visit to Corinth

Timothy returns from Corinth and brings Erastus back with him. Timothy tells Paul that his letter (CORINTHIANS B) has been rejected. Tragically, there is a strong-willed brother in the church who defies Paul's apostolic authority and persuades most of the church to follow his line of thinking.

Upon hearing this news, Paul pays an urgent visit to Corinth. But the visit turns out to be extremely painful. The strong-willed brother defies Paul's apostolic authority in Paul's presence. And the others do not defend Paul in the midst of the man's accusations.

Paul leaves Corinth angry and deeply humiliated. He wants to visit Corinth again and try to correct the problem, but he chooses not to lest he experience sorrow a second time.[47] In haste, he writes a severe letter and gives it to Titus to read to the church. We will call it CORINTHIANS C. This letter no longer exists.[48]

PAUL WRITES CORINTHIANS C

(This letter is lost to us.)

Year: A.D. 55
From: Ephesus
To: The church in Corinth (which is about 5 years old)
Provocation: After returning from Corinth in anger, Paul composes this stinging and severe letter to the Corinthians. He writes it in pure agony and bathes it in tears. In the letter, Paul asks the church to prove its love for him by disciplining the man who has defied his authority.

As soon as Titus goes off to Corinth with the letter, Paul regrets writing it. He fears that its severe tone may exacerbate the situation. Paul is heartbroken and worried over the Corinthian church.

Opposition in Ephesus
June 57

Paul is plotting his next move. He plans to leave Ephesus and visit the churches in Macedonia (Philippi, Thessalonica, and Berea) and Corinth. He then plans to bring the relief fund from these churches to Jerusalem, after which he plans to visit Rome. Paul sends Timothy and Erastus ahead of him to prepare for his arrival in Macedonia.[49]

Paul's influence in Ephesus causes many in the city to forsake their idols. As a result, the silversmiths who make their living selling miniature statues of the Greek goddess Diana (also called Artemis, the goddess of fertility) are losing customers.

Demetrius, one of the silversmiths, calls his fellow silversmiths together and spearheads a mob protest against Paul. Demetrius convinces the silversmiths that Paul is hurting their business by discrediting the temple of the Great Diana. Upon hearing this, the mob is filled with fury and screams out, "Great is Diana of the Ephesians!"

The protest bleeds throughout the city, causing a massive uproar. The protesters move into the Ephesian amphitheater, which holds 25,000 people. In a ranting rage, the mob seizes Aristarchus and Gaius.[50] Paul wants to go into the theater to confront the mob, but the Ephesian believers prevent him. Even some officials of the province (also called *asiarchs*), who are Paul's friends, send him a message begging him not to go into the theater.

The Jews from Ephesus wish to dissociate themselves from Paul, so they have a Jew named Alexander speak on their behalf. When the Ephesians realize that Alexander is a Jew—knowing that Jews do not worship pagan gods—the crowd shouts continually for two hours, "Great is Diana of the Ephesians!" After several hours of mayhem, the town clerk calms the mob down and suggests that those who have a complaint against Paul go through the proper governmental channels to resolve it. The clerk then dismisses the crowd.[51]

It is here that Paul drops to the lowest point of his life. The opposition from Ephesian "wild beasts" (as he calls them metaphorically) is so great that Paul falls into despair.[52] The plots of the Jews have severely tried him.[53] He describes himself as feeling "pressed out of measure," "despairing even of life," "having the sentence of death" upon me. The human hostility from Paul's "many adversaries" is so arduous that Paul comes close to dying. But God delivers him.[54] (During this period of time, Priscilla and Aquila risk their necks for the apostle.)[55]

Back in nearby Colosse, Epaphras plants three churches in the south banks of the Lycus valley: One in Colosse (his hometown), one in Laodicea, and one in Hierapolis.[56]

From Ephesus to Troas

Before leaving Ephesus, Paul sends for the Ephesian believers to secretly meet him somewhere in the city. The meeting is held and Paul speaks words of encouragement to the church, says good-bye, and heads out for Troas.

In Troas, Paul is given an open door to preach the gospel, and he plants a church in that city. A community expressing God's nature is born in Troas! Tragically, Paul's mind is still unsettled about the Corinthian church. He desperately hopes to see Titus and find out how the Corinthians received his "severe letter." Paul searches for Titus throughout Troas, but he fails to find him. Paul is so burdened about the church at Corinth that he leaves Troas despite the open door that God has given him. He sets out for Macedonia where he will look for Titus.[57]

As Paul travels to Macedonia, he fights fears within his own heart about the Corinthian church. When he arrives in the province, he receives opposition. Yet in spite of it, Paul encourages the three Macedonian churches (Philippi, Thessalonica, and Berea).[58] Paul exhorts each of the churches to continue collecting for the Jerusalem relief fund, and boasts in the example set by the church in Corinth...for they have been zealous in laying up for their collection for the past year.[59]

As Paul visits each church, the Holy Spirit reveals to him through various believers that tribulation and imprisonment await him in Jerusalem.[60]

Finally, Paul finds Titus in Macedonia with good news from Corinth. Paul's severe letter has been received! The Corinthians have repented and have taken action! The church disciplined the man who defied the apostle's spiritual authority. But it was too extreme in its discipline.[61] Titus tells Paul that the church treated him (Titus) with great respect and humility. He also tells him that Corinth has slacked off in collecting money for the relief fund.[62] Paul is comforted by the report and begins writing the church another letter.[63] We will call it CORINTHIANS D. This is our 2 Corinthians.

While Paul is writing this letter, he gets word that the church in Corinth is having a new problem. Not long after Titus left Corinth, the church was visited by Jewish "super apostles" (as Paul sarcastically calls them) who undermine Paul's authority and seek to bring the Corinthians under the authority of the Jerusalem church.[64]

Regrettably, some of the Corinthians have received these men and their false gospel—which is a gospel of Law. The "super apostles" try to discredit Paul in the eyes of the Corinthians by telling them the following:

- Paul cannot be trusted. He is not a man of his word. Example: He changed his mind regarding his travel plans. He says one thing but does another. Therefore, his "yes" does not mean "yes," and his "no" does not mean "no."
- When Paul preached to you, he left out the most glorious and life-giving part of the gospel…the Law.
- Paul is not a real apostle. He does not have a letter of commendation like we (the "super apostles") have nor does he accept money for himself. If he were a real apostle, he would have a letter of commendation, and he would take your money.
- Paul is exploiting you by asking you to collect money for a supposed relief fund.
- When Paul is among you, he is weak, humble, and unimpressive in his speaking. But when he is upset, he becomes bold, fierce, and articulate in his letters.
- Paul does not have supernatural experiences like we (the "super apostles") have.
- Paul does not possess the impeccable Israelite pedigree that we (the "super apostles") have.[65]

PAUL WRITES CORINTHIANS D
(This is our 2 Corinthians.)

Year: A.D. 57
From: Macedonia
To: The church in Corinth (which is about 6 years old)
Provocation: Paul encourages the church to forgive the man who defied him. He shares his heart about why he wrote the "painful" letter (CORINTHIANS C). Paul responds to the charge that his word cannot be trusted and clarifies why he changed his travel plans (chapters 1-2). (The letter digresses into a parenthesis from 2:14 to 7:4.) He responds to the charge that he has no letter of commendation and compares his life-giving gospel with the death-giving gospel of his opponents (chapters 3-4). Paul exhorts the

believers to not yoke themselves with unbelievers and becomes very autobiographical about his emotions behind writing the severe letter. In doing so, he exhorts the church to be reconciled to him and to the Lord (chapters 5-7). Paul then encourages the church to resume the collection for the Jerusalem relief fund (chapters 8-9). He urges Titus to visit the church along with another brother "whose fame in the gospel has spread to all the churches" (probably Luke) to help the Corinthians complete the collection. Titus and Luke willingly accept Paul's appeal. In the last three chapters (chapters 10-13), Paul addresses the major charges the Jewish "super apostles" have employed in an effort to take over the Corinthian church. To Paul, the process of defending his apostleship is utter foolishness. But he does so anyway to save the church from accepting a false gospel. And in doing so, he exposes the fleshliness of the "super apostles" in very strong terms. Paul sends the letter with Titus and Luke.

Stop and read 2 Corinthians

Paul leaves Macedonia and brings the gospel "as far as Illyricum."[66] Illyricum is a large mountainous region northwest of Macedonia on the east of the Adriatic Sea. The Roman province called Dalmatia is a reference to the same place.[67] (Illyricum covers the modern regions of Albania, Yugoslavia, and Croatia.) After founding a Christian community in Illyricum, Paul returns to Macedonia.

A Winter in Corinth
Winter 57

Paul leaves Macedonia and visits the church in Corinth for the third time.[68] He spends three winter months with the church and stays in the home of Gaius Titius Justus.[69] Paul is pleased to learn that the Corinthians have received his last letter, and they have completed their collection for the relief fund.[70]

Paul is in contact with Priscilla and Aquila, who are in Rome, and gets word that the faith and witness of the Roman church is spreading all over the world. Not a few travelers who have visited the Eternal City have come to Christ, and they have taken their new faith to their homelands. Paul longs to see the church in Rome. He has tried to visit Rome on many occasions, but he has been hindered every time.

Priscilla and Aquila ask Paul to pen a full proclamation of the gospel for the visitors who come to the Lord in Rome and leave the city. They also tell him about the tension that exists between the Jews and the Gentiles in the church. The two groups are disputing over the issues of meat-eating and keeping holy days.

Specifically, there are those in the church who are "weak in conscience" (Jews) who believe that eating meat is sin.[71] They also feel that they must keep certain days holy, as prescribed in the Law. These "weak" scrupulous brethren are judging and criticizing their emancipated (Gentile) brethren who have liberty in these areas. The emancipated believers, who have a "strong" conscience in these matters, are looking down upon and despising their weaker scrupulous brethren.

In addition, there are some who have come into the church who are causing divisions. Such are slaves to their own fleshly appetites, deceivers who are speaking against the gospel that Paul brings.[72]

Paul's eight coworkers join Paul in Corinth and bring him the collection for the Jerusalem relief fund from their respective churches. The men make plans to accompany Paul to Jerusalem to deliver the relief fund.[73] Luke leaves Corinth and returns to Philippi.

PAUL WRITES ROMANS

Year: Winter 57

From: Corinth

To: The church of Rome (which is about 3 years old)

Provocation: This letter has three purposes: 1) *An apostolic purpose:* To gain support from the Roman church for Paul's trip to Spain. 2) *An apologetic purpose:* To give a clear setting forth of the gospel of grace, and to develop a defense of God's righteousness in the gospel which is under attack, and 3) *A pastoral purpose:* To deal with the problems of division within the church between the Jewish and Gentile believers. Romans is written in the form of rhetoric called "diatribe"—a style of writing where the author raises objections and then answers them. In chapters 1-5, Paul masterfully presents the gospel of Jesus Christ as it relates to justification and the forgiveness of sins. In chapters 6-8, he discusses sanctification and deliverance from sin and the Law. In chapters 9-11, Paul explains the role of Israel in God's purpose. In chapters 12-16, he addresses the problems the Gentile believers are having with the Jewish believers on the subject of meat-eating and holy days. In these latter chapters, he addresses every problem he has seen a church have throughout his long experience as a church planter. Paul closes the letter by sharing his desire to bring the gospel to the westernmost country in the Roman Empire, Spain. On his way there, he hopes to visit the Roman church. But before he does, Paul intends to go to Jerusalem to deliver the relief fund. He asks for their prayers—for he knows that he will face danger from the Jews in the holy city and does not want his plans to see the Romans to be thwarted. Paul closes the letter by sending greetings from various members of the Corinthian church as well as from some of his apostolic coworkers who are with him. Tertius, a brother in the church in Corinth, pens the letter for Paul. The letter is delivered by Phoebe, a servant in the church in Cenchrea. (Being so close to Corinth—seven miles east—the church in Cenchrea was no doubt born as a natural outgrowth of the Corinthian church.)

Stop and read Romans

From Troas to Miletus
Spring 58

After three months in Corinth, Paul wishes to head east and return to Antioch, Syria, but the Jews hatch a plot to kill him. So he heads north to Philippi in Macedonia. In Philippi, Paul picks up Luke and sends his eight coworkers ahead of him to Troas where he and Luke will join them.

Paul and Luke visit Neapolis,[74] then sail off to Troas. The trip takes them five days because of unfavorable winds. They come to Troas where Paul's eight apprentices are waiting for him. Paul and his companions will spend a week with the Christian community in Troas.[75]

The church in Troas gathers on Sunday evenings to break bread. The believers meet on the third floor of an *insula* that is lit with many torches. The air in the room is smokey and stuffy.

Paul gathers with the church on Sunday evening to break bread. Seeking to leave the next day, he preaches until midnight. A young boy between the ages of eight and fourteen named Eutychus is sitting on a ledge. The smoke from the torches causes Eutychus to become sleepy. While

Paul continues to preach, Eutychus falls asleep and drops out of the window to his death. Paul runs down to where the boy is and throws himself on his body, putting his arms around him. Paul tells those around him to be calm for the boy is alive. Eutychus gets up and takes the Lord's Supper with the rest of the church. After the believers eat, Paul continues to speak to them until dawn.[76]

The next morning, Paul's eight coworkers and Luke set sail ahead of Paul to Assos. Paul chooses not to sail, but to travel by land. He meets the others in Assos, from which they all sail to Mitylene. The next day they arrive in Kios. The day after, they come to Samos. The following day they harbor at Miletus, which is located 30 miles south of Ephesus.[77] (Paul chooses to sail past Ephesus as he wants to make it to Jerusalem for the day of Pentecost.) Paul sends word to the Ephesian elders to meet him in Miletus.

The Ephesian elders arrive, and Paul gives them a very moving farewell speech. He tells the elders of his plans to visit Jerusalem, not knowing what his fate will be there. He warns the elders that wolves will emerge from within and from without the church. These wolves will bring perverse teachings in order to draw disciples after themselves.

Paul charges the elders to feed and guard the flock of God from such people and to work with their own hands—for it is better to give than to receive. Paul tells the elders that they will never see his face again.

As Paul closes his farewell speech, he kneels down and prays with the elders. They all break out into loud weeping and embrace Paul, covering him with kisses. (Paul's statement that he will never see them again grieves the elders terribly.)[78] The elders escort Paul to the ship.

Paul and his company leave Miletus by ship and follow a straight course, passing through Cos, Rhodes, and Patara. In Patara, they find a ship crossing over to Phoenicia. They board it and set sail across the Mediterranean Sea to Tyre in Palestine, where the ship stops to unload cargo. The trip from Patara to Tyre lasts five days.

The men meet with the church in Tyre for a week. (The church in Tyre was founded during the dispersion after Stephen's martyrdom.) Some brethren in Tyre prophesy that tribulation awaits Paul in Jerusalem, so they urge him not to set foot there. The whole church, including the women and children, escorts Paul and his companions out of the city. They all kneel down on the beach and pray, bidding each other a loving farewell.[79]

A Visit to Caesarea

Paul and his companions board ship and head south to the seaport town of Ptolemais, where they spend a day with the church in that town.

They then head off to Caesarea, the home of Philip the evangelist. Paul and his company stay with Philip and his four unmarried daughters, who are all prophetesses.[80]

While in Caesarea, Agabus (from Jerusalem) pays Paul a visit. In OT-prophet fashion, Agabus dramatically prophesies that the Jews in Jerusalem will bind Paul and hand him to the Gentiles. He takes Paul's girdle and binds his own hands and feet with it while uttering this prediction.

Upon hearing this prophecy, the believers weep and beg Paul not to go to Jerusalem. But Paul cannot be persuaded. He tells them he is ready to die in Jerusalem for the name of Jesus Christ. The church stops pressing Paul and says, "The will of the Lord be done."

Paul, Luke, and the eight coworkers head off to Jerusalem with the relief fund. Jerusalem is a 64-mile trip from Caesarea. It is about a three-day walk. Some of the brothers from the church in Caesarea accompany the men to Jerusalem.[81]

Troubles in Jerusalem

Paul and his company arrive in Jerusalem. The church receives them gladly. Since many of the Jews in the church in Jerusalem have a problem hosting Paul's Gentile companions, the Caesarean brethren take Paul and his company to the home of Mnason, a Gentile in the church at Jerusalem, where the men stay. (Mnason is from Cyprus and has been a Christian in the church in Jerusalem from the beginning.)

The next day Paul and his companions appear before James (the Lord's half-brother) and the Jerusalem elders. Paul greets them and testifies about what God has done among the Gentiles through his ministry. He then hands the relief fund to the elders. The elders rejoice and give glory to God.[82]

The elders inform Paul that thousands of Jews have believed on the Lord in Jerusalem, and they all are zealous for the Law. These Jews have heard false rumors that he teaches the Jews living in Gentile lands to disobey the Law of Moses and disregard the ancient Jewish customs. Therefore, Paul is *persona non grata* in Jerusalem, by both the believing Jews and the Jews of the city as a whole. Accordingly, his life is in danger.

The elders have tried to dispel this rumor, but they ask Paul to do something himself to demonstrate that he is a practicing Jew. They suggest that Paul take part in a Nazarite purification ceremony along with four other Jewish believers.[83] Paul agrees and shaves his head for the purification rite. He also pays the expenses of the other four men to have their heads shaved.[84]

The next day, Paul purifies himself with the four Jewish brethren and they walk to the temple together. After seven days, some Jews from Ephesus who are visiting Jerusalem for Pentecost see Paul in the temple with the four men. They remember Paul from when he was in Ephesus and they believe that he is an enemy of the Law of Moses.

Because these men had seen Paul and Trophimus walk together in Jerusalem earlier, they mistakenly assume that Paul took Trophimus into the temple. So they shout aloud, "Men of Israel, this is the man who teaches against the Law of Moses everywhere, and he has come here and taken Gentiles into the sacred temple!" (It is a capital offense for a Gentile to enter the temple area. Gentiles are limited to an area outside the temple called "the court of the Gentiles.")[85] Immediately, the city goes into turmoil.

In a mad rush, the Jews seize Paul, drag him out of the temple, shut the doors, and begin beating him. The Roman commander (also called *tribune*), Claudius Lysias, gets word of what is happening and sends soldiers to rescue Paul from the angry mob.

When the Jews see the Roman commander and his soldiers, they immediately stop beating Paul. The soldiers arrest Paul, chaining both his hands. They ask who Paul is and what he has done. The crowd begins to shout out different answers so that the soldiers cannot get a clear answer. The commander orders the soldiers to take Paul to the Antonia fortress (also called "the barracks"). The soldiers carry him into the fortress because of the violence of the crowd. (The fortress is connected to the outer court of the temple by just two flights of steps. The fortress overlooks the temple area.) The crowd screams, "Away with him!"

When Paul gets to the fortress, he asks the commander permission to address the Jewish crowd. When the commander discovers that Paul speaks Greek, he grants him permission. (The commander is surprised that Paul speaks Greek, because he wrongly assumes that Paul is the Egyptian revolutionary who is hated by the Jews.)[86]

Paul stands on the steps of the fortress and motions with his hands for the crowd to be quiet. When the crowd falls silent, Paul begins to address them in the Hebrew tongue. He begins by sharing the testimony of his life as a Pharisee and how he became a follower of Jesus. The Jews listen to him until he tells them that God sent him to the Gentiles, at which point they then begin to shout, "Rid the earth of him! He is not fit to live!" The crowd is yelling, waving their garments and flinging dust into the air.

The Roman soldiers assume that Paul is intentionally instigating the crowd (for they cannot understand Hebrew). So they get ready to interrogate him by flogging. This brutal innovation could result in crippling or even death before the truth has been arrived at! When Paul makes the soldiers aware that he is a Roman citizen, the centurion drops the scourge and tells the Roman commander that Paul is a citizen. The Roman commander verifies that this is true. Consequently, Paul is not flogged. (It is unlawful for a Roman citizen to be flogged without a trial.)

The next day, the Roman commander releases Paul and orders the chief priests and the Sanhedrin to hold a trial for him. When the Sanhedrin comes together, Paul fixes his eyes on the judges and opens by saying that he has lived in all good conscience before God until the present day. Ananias, the high priest, orders Paul to be struck across the mouth, for such a statement is blasphemous. Paul retorts that God will strike Ananias. After insulting the high priest, Paul continues with his defense.

Noting that one half of the Sanhedrin is made up of Sadducees and the other half is made up of Pharisees, Paul throws a theological curve ball into the midst of the Sanhedrin. He declares that he is a Pharisee, the son of a Pharisee, and that he is on trial for believing in the resurrection of the dead! (The Sadducees and Pharisees are bitterly divided on this point of doctrine. The Pharisees believe in the resurrection while the Sadducees deny it.)

Immediately, a dispute breaks out in the Sanhedrin. The Pharisees claim that they find nothing wrong with Paul, and that perhaps an angel has spoken to him. The dispute becomes so heated that the Roman soldiers remove Paul and bring him back to the fortress for fear that the Sadducees will tear him apart.

The next night, the Lord Jesus appears to Paul and stands over him. The Lord tells him to take courage and that he will bear testimony for Him in Rome just as he did in Jerusalem.[87]

Bound to Caesarea

At daybreak, more than 40 Jews meet together and plot to assassinate Paul. They bind themselves by an oath to forfeit food and drink until he is dead. These Jews approach the Sanhedrin with their plans and the Sanhedrin is supportive.

Paul's nephew hears of the plot and reports it to Paul, who is still being held in the fortress. Paul has his nephew tell the Roman commander of the plot. When the Roman commander learns of it, he orders 470 heavily armed troops to secretly take Paul to Caesarea in the middle of the night. (The 470 is made up of 200 soldiers, 70 horsemen, and 200 spearmen.)[88] Paul is guarded and in chains. The Roman commander writes a letter to

Felix, the governor of Caesarea, and rehearses to him why he is sending Paul into his custody.

Paul spends only twelve days in Jerusalem before he is taken to Caesarea, which is located 64 miles northwest of Jerusalem.[89]

ENDNOTES

1. 1 Corinthians 16:1. We do not have this letter, nor do we know exactly when Paul told the Galatians about the relief fund.

2. Timothy is the exception. He is half Jewish and half Gentile.

3. Romans 15:24ff.

4. Romans 16:5 says that Epaenetus is "the first convert to Christ from Asia" (NASB).

5. Alexandria is the second largest city in the Empire, next to Rome. Its population at this time is about 600,000. It has a large Jewish population of 200,000.

6. Apollos was probably schooled in the allegorical style of expositing the Bible pioneered by Philo of Alexandria, the famed Jewish philosopher. This theory has led some scholars to suggest that Apollos wrote the Book of Hebrews, which resonates with Philo's style of allegorical interpretation.

7. According to the Western Text, Apollos came to the Lord in his home city of Alexandria. There was a Jewish Christian community in Alexandria as early as A.D. 41. In that year, Emperor Claudius wrote to the Greeks and Jews in Alexandria because of civil strife they were experiencing over Christianity, which he calls a "general plague which infests the whole world."

8. It is possible that the gospel reached Alexandria after Pentecost by those who had lived there, came to Jerusalem, and returned. This may have been the way that Apollos had heard it.

9. This is the story according to the Western Text.

10. Acts 18:24ff; 1 Corinthians 1:12–3:22.

11. 1 Corinthians 1:17-25.

12. According to 1 Corinthians 9:6, the Corinthians are familiar with Barnabas. So he must have visited them.

13. 1 Corinthians 9:5.

14. 1 Corinthians 1:12; 3:22; 9:5. Peter is called "Cephas" in these passages.

15. 1 Corinthians 1:22.

16. 1 Corinthians 1:12-13; 3:4-9,21-23.

17. In certain Greek texts, Sopater is said to be the son of Pyrrhus.

18. Aristarchus may be a Jew (see Colossians 4:10-11).

19. While Luke does not explicitly tell us that Paul picked these men up to go with him to Ephesus, we know they are there in Ephesus with him. The following passages of Scripture put all eight men in Ephesus

during the time that Paul was there: Acts 19:22; 20:4; 21:29; 1 Corinthians 4:17; 16:10,20 (Paul wrote 1 Corinthians from Ephesus). One can infer that Titus is there since Luke never mentions him throughout Acts, yet we know he is present on many occasions from Paul's letters. We learn from 2 Corinthians 8 that Titus represented Corinth for the Jerusalem relief fund, and it is clear from the letter to Titus that Paul trained him.

20. For a discussion on the biblical and historical evidence showing that Paul trained men in Ephesus, see *So You Want to Start a House Church?*, Chapters 1 and 3.

21. According to the Western Text, Paul had use of the building for these hours. Further, the hours between 11 a.m. and 4 p.m. are when public affairs such as schooling and judicial activities come to a halt in all Greco-Roman cities. Thus Tyrannus' hall was not in use then.

22. Acts 19:1-10; 20:4.

23. Acts 20:34; 1 Corinthians 4:11-12.

24. Acts 20:20; 1 Corinthians 16:19.

25. 1 Corinthians 16:9.

26. 2 Corinthians 11:28.

27. Acts 20:27.

28. Acts 20:31.

29. Acts 19:10.

30. Acts 20:31.

31 Nero's madness was mostly kept in check by the guidance of philosopher Seneca and Burrus (head of the praetorian guard). In A.D. 62, Seneca retired and Burrus died, and the madness of Nero was fully unleashed. In A.D. 65, Nero ordered Seneca to commit suicide.

32. The Greek drachma (silver coin) is the value of a day's wage, the equivalent of the Roman denarius.

33. Acts 19:11-20.

34 Sosthenes is present with Paul when Paul writes 1 Corinthians (1Corinthians 1:1).

35. 1 Corinthians 5:9-13.

36. 2 Corinthians 8:6.

37. Paul had just finished writing 1 Corinthans 1–4 when the three Corinthian brothers abruptly visited him. The wording in chapter 5:1 suggests that Paul had just received the news about the illicit sexual relations in the church, and he responded to it immediately.

38. In the first century, the Lord's Supper was a full meal (see *Rethinking the Wineskin*, Chapter 2).

39. Like all Romans, the Corinthians ate while reclining on couches, usually situated in a U shape (called a *triclinium*) around a low table. (Corinth is a Roman colony, so Roman customs are observed.) Diners supported their body weight with their left elbows and ate with their right fingers. The common banquet etiquette of the first century was to separate those who ate by social class. The wealthy merchants were fed with one kind of food in the dining room (*triclinium*). About nine to twelve people could fit there. The leftovers and less superior foods were given to the poor and slaves in the courtyard (*atrium*).

40. The Greco-Roman world had an acute shortage of women. Roman women married in their early to mid-teens. (Men waited to marry until their mid-twenties.) The legal minimum age for marriage was twelve. Both Roman and Jewish marriages were typically arranged by the parents of the prospective spouses. When a woman married, she wore a veil in public. The veil was a social indicator that a woman was married. An unveiled woman signified to others that she was unmarried. Thus for married women to wear veils in public was a matter of decorum and supreme importance in Roman society. Married women who did not wear veils in public settings were viewed as shaming their husbands and portraying themselves as promiscuous wives, i.e. unashamed adulteresses. In 44 B.C., a "new" type of woman emerged in Rome. By the first century, these "new women" had spread throughout the Roman Empire. The "new women" were liberated married women who pursued their social lives at the expense of their families and who defied previously accepted norms of marriage fidelity and chastity. They were sexually promiscuous and dressed in a seductive manner. Because Paul was a liberator of women, it is not difficult to see that some Christian women associated his views on a woman's freedom with the immoral ideals of the "new women." For a detailed discussion on the cultural meaning of the marriage veil in the first century and "the new Roman women," see Bruce Winter's *After Paul Left Corinth* (Eerdmans), Chapter 6 and his *Roman Wives, Roman Widows: The Appearance of New Women and the Pauline Communities* (Eerdmans), Chapter 5.

41. Those with a higher social status did not typically dine in the *tabernae* (taverns). They instead dined in pagan temples, which included dining with the pagan god itself. Sometimes a statue of the god would be placed on a separate couch as if he were dining with the feasters. And a prayer would be offered to the god before the meal.

42. Well-to-do Greeks despised common labor and looked down on those who engaged in it. This would include those who worked as

leatherworkers and tentmakers. To such ones Paul lost credibility because he worked with his hands and did not take money for his teaching as the Sophists did.

43. This scenario is derived from mirror-reading Paul's words in 1 Corinthians.

44. For a discussion on the biblical and historical evidence demonstrating how Paul planted the Roman church, see *So You Want to Start a House Church?*, Chapter 1.

45. According to Romans 16, Paul greets twenty-six individuals and five households who are gathering in Rome. Though Paul had not visited Rome yet, he knows all of these people by name.

46. Adronicus and Junias, relatives of Paul, are said to be Paul's fellow prisoners at one time. We do not know when or where this would have happened.

47. 2 Corinthians 1:22–2:4; 12:21.

48. 2 Corinthians 2:4ff; 7:8ff.

49. Acts 19:21-22.

50. It is my view that the Gaius here is the Gaius from Derbe (Acts 20:4). Some manuscripts refer to Aristarchus and Gaius as "men from Macedonia" while others use the singular form, Gaius and Aristarchus, "a man from Macedonia."

51. Acts 19:23-41.

52. 1 Corinthians 15:32. The reference to "wild beasts" may refer to human opposition. However, there is a long-standing tradition among Greek writers where human passions and pleasures of the flesh are described as beasts that fight against man. In the context of 1 Corinthians 15:32, Paul may have had this in mind.

53. Acts 20:19.

54. 2 Corinthians 1:8-10; 1 Corinthians 16:8-9.

55. Romans 16:3-4. We can only speculate as to how they did this; Paul does not say.

56. This scenario is derived from mirror-reading Paul's statement about Philemon, Epaphras, and Onesimus in his letters to the Colossians and Philemon. Neither Colosse, Laodicea, nor Hierapolis are Roman colonies. The Lycus valley has a large Jewish population. It is part of Phrygia Asiana as opposed to Phrygia Galatica, where the four Galatian churches are located.

57. 2 Corinthians 2:12-13; Acts 20:5-7.

58. Acts 20:3; 2 Corinthians 7:5-6.

59. 2 Corinthians 9:2.

60. Acts 20:23.

61. 2 Corinthians 2:1-11; 7:6-7.

62. 2 Corinthians 8:6-11.

63. 2 Corinthians 7:13-16.

64. This is a clear breach of the agreement that Paul and Barnabas made with Peter, James, and John (see Galatians 2:8-9).

65. This scenario is derived from mirror-reading Paul's words in 2 Corinthians.

66. Romans 15:19.

67. 2 Timothy 4:10.

68. 2 Corinthians 12:14; 13:1.

69. Romans 16:23.

70. 2 Corinthians 8:6ff.

71. No doubt because these Jewish Christians were trying to avoid eating meats that had been sacrificed to pagan gods or that were not properly slaughtered according to Jewish law.

72. This scenario is derived from mirror-reading Paul's words in Romans.

73. Acts 20:1-4.

74. Inferred from Acts 16:11.

75. Acts 20:1-6.

76. Acts 20:4-12.

77. In the second century B.C. the population of Miletus is estimated at 100,000. It is doubtful if the size of the city increased greatly under the Roman Empire.

78. Acts 20:13-38.

79. Acts 21:1-6.

80. According to the church historian Eusebius, Philip and at least three of his daughters migrated to Hierapolis in Asia Minor where they died. At least one of the daughters got married.

81. Acts 21:7-16.

82. Acts 24:17. Since Luke never mentions the relief fund in Acts and Paul does not mention its effect in his "Captivity Letters" (the epistles he wrote after he was imprisoned in Rome), we may assume that the fund did not have the kind of effect that Paul wanted it to have—namely, the uniting of the Jewish and Gentile churches.

83. 1 Corinthians 9:20.

84. The purification rite is the Nazarite vow discussed in Numbers 6.

85. An inscription on the temple clearly warned that any Gentile—including any Roman citizen—who violated the sacred area would be put to immediate death by stoning.

86. Three years previously an Egyptian revolutionary who claimed to be a prophet came to Jerusalem. He led a large band of followers to the Mount of Olives and told them to wait for his word of command. The walls of the city would fall flat and they would overthrow the Roman garrison and take the city. Governor Felix, however, sent troops in and killed some of them and imprisoned others. The Egyptian discreetly escaped and became the rage of many of the Jews in Jerusalem. The Roman commander thought that Paul was this Egyptian.

87. Acts 21:17–23:11.

88. Given the Roman-Jewish unrest that was building in Judea at this time, the Roman commander called for a strong military response to stave off any explosive and devastating uprising that would result from Paul's ambush.

89. Acts 23:12-35.

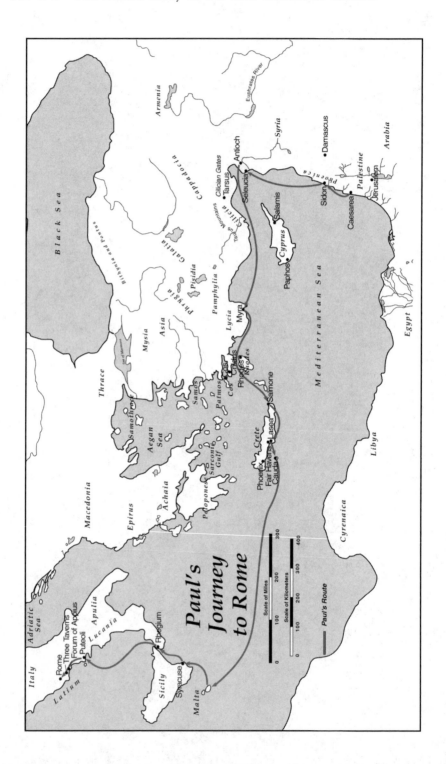

Chapter 12

The Roman Chronicle

A.D. 59–A.D. 62

Then he stayed two whole years in his own rented house. And he welcomed all who visited him, proclaiming the kingdom of God and teaching the things concerning the Lord Jesus Christ with full boldness and without hindrance (Acts 28:30-31).

Paul's Caesarean Imprisonment
Summer 59

Caesarea is a predominantly Gentile city. It is the Roman headquarters of Judea. Paul is placed in custody in the governor's palace and guarded by a Roman centurion. Paul will spend two years here.

Felix is the governor of the province. Paul is presented to Felix, and Felix reads the letter written about Paul by the Roman commander. Felix promises Paul a fair hearing and detains him in Herod's praetorium (the governor's palace).

Five days following his arrival in Caesarea, Paul appears before Ananias the high priest and some Jewish elders who travel to Caesarea to examine Paul. The Jews bring an orator named Tertullus to prosecute Paul before Felix. When Tertullus finishes his prosecution, Felix asks Paul to respond.

Paul defends his actions and points out that no witnesses are present to accuse him. Felix is persuaded by Paul's point and announces that his case will be decided when Claudius Lysias (the Roman commander) arrives.

Felix orders that Paul be kept in guarded custody in the governor's palace. Paul's friends are given permission to care for his needs. From time to time, Felix calls for Paul, and Paul shares Jesus Christ with him. When Paul discusses the judgment of God, however, Felix becomes fearful and leaves. Felix hopes that Paul will offer him a bribe, but he never does. Felix never releases Paul because he wants to gain favor from the Jews.[1] As a result, Paul spends two years in prison in Caesarea.[2]

Spring 60

Porcius Festus replaces Felix as governor. Three days after arriving in the province, Festus pays a visit to Jerusalem. While Festus is there, the Jerusalem Jews request that Paul be brought to trial in Jerusalem. (The reason why they asked this favor is because they planned to ambush Paul and kill him on his way.)

Festus tells the Jews to send their leading men to Caesarea and make their accusations against Paul there. Eight to ten days later, Festus returns to Caesarea and has Paul brought before him. The case is reopened. A deputation of the Sanhedrin arrives in Caesarea and levels accusations against Paul before Festus, none of which they can prove. Paul states that he has done nothing wrong to the Jews, to the temple, to the Law, or to Caesar.

Festus, wanting to do the Jews a favor, asks Paul if he is willing to go to Jerusalem to stand trial before the Sanhedrin. Paul knows that if he agrees, the Jews will try to take his life. So he exercises his right as a Roman citizen and appeals to Caesar in Rome. Legally, Festus must comply. So he does.

In order for Festus to send Paul to Rome, he must write and send a letter with the accused. The letter must outline the nature of the case and the course of events that led up to it. King Agrippa, who is ruler of part of Northern Palestine, and his sister Bernice are visiting Caesarea at this time. Agrippa is well-versed in the Jewish religion. Since Festus is unclear about Jewish law and does not know how to write a letter about Paul's case, he rehearses Paul's situation before King Agrippa. Upon hearing the case, Agrippa requests to hear Paul for himself.

The next day Paul is brought before King Agrippa and Bernice, giving his defense at a judicial hearing. When Paul finishes, Festus shouts, "You are crazy, Paul. It is all your learning that has made you crazy!" Agrippa, however, finds Paul's testimony rather persuasive. Agrippa concludes that Paul has done nothing worthy of death or imprisonment. But he cannot release Paul because Paul has already appealed to Caesar.[3]

Paul's Voyage to Rome

Paul and some other prisoners are placed into the custody of a Roman centurion named Julius, who is part of the Imperial Regiment. The prisoners are guarded by Roman soldiers. Luke from Antioch and

Aristarchus from Thessalonica accompany Paul on the voyage. Luke passes as the ship's doctor, and Aristarchus passes as Paul's servant.[4] They
board a coasting vessel about to sail for ports along the coast of the
province of Asia.

The next day the ship stops in Sidon. (It is 67 miles from Caesarea
to Sidon.) Julius, the centurion, treats Paul kindly and allows him to visit
the church in that city. From Sidon, the ship sails east and north of Cyprus
because the prevailing winds are moving westward. They then sail across
the open sea along the coasts of Cilicia and Pamphylia and stop at Myra
in Lycia.[5] (The trip from Sidon to Myra is over 400 miles.)

In Myra, the centurion finds a grain ship of Alexandria sailing to
Italy. The men set sail on the Alexandrian ship with 276 other passengers.
The winds are unfavorable and the ship moves slowly through Cnidus,
along Crete, and stops at Fair Havens, near the city of Lasea, waiting for
the wind to change.

Sailing is now dangerous and Paul offers his advice to the centurion.
He predicts that if the crew leaves now, the voyage will lead to a shipwreck. The centurion does not regard Paul's advice. He rather listens to
the judgment of the steersman who advises that they put out to sea and
stop in Phoenix, the harbor of Crete, for the winter.

The Shipwreck

While they are coasting along the shore of Crete a furious northeast-
er wind called *Euraquilo* catches the ship, causing great damage and fear.
Not long after, a major shipwreck ensues.[6] An angel appears to Paul and
tells him not to be afraid for he (Paul) will stand in the presence of Caesar. The angel also tells Paul that God has granted that he (Paul) and the
lives of the entire crew will be spared. Paul encourages the crew with this
news and gives them practical direction during the crisis.

The ship is utterly destroyed, and the passengers almost lose their
lives. Yet they all escape unharmed as Paul predicted. Paul shows himself
to be a very practical and bold man in the midst of major crisis.[7]

Wintering in Malta
A.D. 60–61

It is morning. The crew arrives safely ashore on an island called Malta.
Malta is only eighteen miles long and eight miles wide. It is located some
60 miles south of Sicily. The crew is wet, cold, hungry, and sick. The natives
of Malta are hospitable and build a fire for the men to warm themselves.

Paul again makes himself useful, gathering brushwood to keep the fire going. As he does, a poisonous snake emerges from the brushwood and bites him on the hand. The natives conclude that Paul is getting Divine justice for some crime he committed. Paul shakes the snake off his hand and is unharmed. Upon seeing that Paul did not swell up or die after watching him a long time after the snakebite, the natives conclude that he must be a god.

Publius, the chief man on the island, takes Paul, Luke, and Aristarchus into his home for three days. Publius' father is sick with dysentery. Paul lays hands on him and prays, and the man is healed. The news of the healing spreads on the island and other sick people come to Paul and are healed.

The entire crew spends three winter months on the Island of Malta. When sailing is no longer a hazard, they set sail for Rome on an Alexandrian ship.[8]

MARK WRITES HIS GOSPEL

Year: A.D. late 50s–early 60s
From: Rome
To: Unknown
Provocation: John Mark's Gospel is based on Peter's account. Mark presents Christ as the Suffering Servant of God.

MATTHEW WRITES HIS GOSPEL

Year: A.D. late 50s–early 60s
From: Antioch of Syria
To: The Jews
Provocation: Matthew presents Christ as the King of the Jews.

LUKE WRITES HIS GOSPEL

Year: A.D. 60-61
From: Rome
To: Theophilus and the Gentiles
Provocation: Luke shares how the gospel, incarnated in Jesus, moved from Galilee to Jerusalem. Luke presents the Humanity of

> Jesus Christ. Theophilus is a patron who finances the publication
> of Luke's two volumes (*Luke-Acts*).

The Roman Christians Greet Paul

The crew stops at Syracuse where they stay for three days. They then arrive in Rhegium. A strong wind propels them to Puteoli, the major port for those traveling to Rome. In Puteoli, Paul and his companions find some believers. The Christians in Puteoli invite Paul to stay with them for seven days. Julius grants him permission to meet with them.

From Puteoli, Paul and his companions are escorted on the Via Appia (also called the Appian Way). The Via Appia is a great Roman road known as "the queen of the long roads." When the church in Rome is alerted that Paul is near the Eternal City, some of the brothers in the church go to a town called Three Taverns (33 miles from Rome) to greet him. Others walk ten miles farther and greet Paul and his companions at the Appian forum.

Upon seeing the Roman believers, Paul is encouraged and gives thanks to God. (Recall that Paul had written the church a letter four years earlier stating his desire to visit the church in Rome. But none of them ever imagined that he would arrive as a prisoner!)

Paul's First Roman Imprisonment

Paul finally arrives in Rome and is placed under house arrest. He lives in his own private lodging on the third floor of a Roman *insula* (apartment) and is chained by his wrist to a Roman guard. The guard is relieved every four hours. Each guard belongs to the Praetorian guard, the emperor's personal bodyguards.[9] Paul will quickly become a talking point among them. Thankfully, Paul is allowed to receive visitors.

On his third day there, Paul invites the local leaders of the Jewish community to visit him. He does this because he cannot attend the synagogue to visit them. When the Jewish leaders arrive, Paul introduces himself and summarizes the course of events that brought him to Rome. The Jewish leaders have never heard of Paul. No one from Judea has written letters about him, and no Jew who has visited Judea has brought back a bad report about him. However, the Jewish leaders are aware of the Christians, for "they are spoken ill of everywhere." They are open to hear Paul's views about the new faith.

At a scheduled day, the Jewish leaders visit Paul (who is still under house arrest) to hear him present the gospel. It is a marathon session, stretching from morning till evening. When Paul is finished, some of the leaders give serious heed to his words, finding them persuasive. Others outright reject his message. Paul announces that he will hereafter preach to the Gentiles because the Gentiles, unlike the Jews, will receive it. The Jewish leaders cannot come to a consensus about Paul's message so they leave.[10]

For the next two years, Paul will carry on the work of preaching and teaching Jesus Christ from his *insula*. Although under house arrest, he welcomes all who visit him, and he enjoys complete freedom of speech.[11]

Paul's imprisonment causes the gospel to advance. First, his personal guards are hearing the message from Paul himself. Second, his imprisonment is giving boldness to some to speak the Word of God without fear. Third, there are some preachers who are jealous of Paul's success in spreading the gospel to so many places in so brief a time. Now that Paul is confined, they feel that they can gain a march on his progress. Paul's response to such ill-motivated souls is that he is happy that Christ is being proclaimed, regardless of the motivation.[12]

Paul is "aged" now. He is about 56 years old, which is very old by first-century standards. He must pay his own rent for his *insula*.[13] Luke and Aristarchus are still with him, tending to his needs.[14] The following men also visit Paul in Rome:

- Tychicus from Ephesus.[15]
- Timothy from Lystra. He will serve as Paul's amanuensis (scribe).[16]
- Demas from Thessalonica.[17]
- John Mark from Jerusalem.[18]

Crisis in Colosse

The church in Colosse is having problems. Some of the believers are not getting along and are mistreating one another. Still worse, false teachers have come into the church and are subverting the gospel of grace. They are introducing a bizarre form of Jewish legalism mixed with a counterfeit spirituality. They are teaching the Colossians the following:

- In order to experience God's "fullness," you must observe the ceremonial laws of the OT. You must observe special "holy" days and eat only "clean" foods. You must also be circumcised.
- Union with God is evidenced by mystical visions and angelic visitations.

- What you handle, taste, and/or touch can either help or harm your union with God. If you handle, taste, or touch that which is "unclean," you will lose your union with God and will never experience His fullness.

The false teaching has also spread to the church in Laodicea. Epaphras, the founder of the Colossian and Laodicean churches, is troubled by this spiritual assault. So he sails to Rome to get advice from Paul. At the same time, Onesimus (Philemon's slave) runs away. But he does not run away empty-handed. He steals money from Philemon! (This is a capital offense.) Epaphras finds Onesimus and takes him to Rome with him, believing that Paul can help him. Onesimus is not a Christian, but he remembers Paul to be a kind man and believes that he will help him.

On his way to Rome to visit Paul, Epaphras (also called Epaphroditus)[19] stops at Philippi to visit the church there. The church in Philippi is greatly encouraged by Epaphras, and it sends him off to Rome with a small fortune as a love offering for Paul. This is the fourth time the church in Philippi has helped Paul monetarily. The Philippians are deeply concerned for Paul and ask Epaphras to let them know how he is doing.

Epaphras and Onesimus continue toward Rome, but Epaphras becomes deathly ill on the way. Yet despite his illness, Epaphras persists on to Rome for the Lord's sake. Onesimus has a message sent to the church in Philippi, letting them know of Epaphras' sickness and requesting prayer for him.

When Epaphras arrives in Rome, he hands Paul the financial gift. He informs Paul of the love the Philippians have for him and gives him an update on their progress.

He also tells him about the church in Colosse. Epaphras joyfully tells him of the love the Colossian believers have for one another. But he also gives Paul a full report of the problems that the churches in Colosse, Laodicea, and Philippi are having. He also lets him know that Archippus—the son of Philemon and Apphia[20]—is deeply discouraged and has stopped ministering to the church in Colosse and Laodicea like he once did.

Upon hearing all the bad news, Paul struggles in prayer for the church in Colosse as well as for the churches in Laodicea and Philippi. Onesimus is with Epaphras, and Paul leads him to Christ. Onesimus turns out to be a real servant to Paul, and Paul grows to depend on him.

When the church in Philippi gets word of Epaphras' sickness, they write Paul a letter inquiring about Epaphras' health. Paul will now write three letters, and he will dictate them all to Timothy to scribe.

Paul will send all three letters by the hand of Tychicus.[21] He instructs Tychicus to encourage the churches and give them an update on his (Paul's) prison situation.[22]

Onesimus will return to Colosse with Tychicus and a letter that Paul will write to Philemon.[23]

PAUL WRITES COLOSSIANS

Year: A.D. 61

From: Rome

To: The church in Colosse (which is about 4 years old)

Provocation: Paul addresses the false gospel that has been introduced in Colosse. He does so by giving the Colossian Christians a peerless unveiling of the cosmic Christ, who is Head of His Body. Paul combats the heresy by declaring that all of God's fullness is in Jesus Christ and that the Colossian believers *already* have union with God through Him, apart from religious works or mystical experiences. Paul ends the letter by exhorting the Colossian Christians to walk in the new man, bearing with one another in love, forgiveness, and respect. He closes by sending greetings from some of the people who are with him and asks the church to read this letter to the church in Laodicea, which gathers in the home of Nympha. In turn, the letter of Laodicea will be sent to the Colossians, and Paul asks that it be read by the Colossian church. (The Laodicean letter is lost to us, but some scholars believe it is our Ephesians.)

Stop and read Colossians

PAUL WRITES PHILEMON

Year: A.D. 61

From: Rome

To: Philemon, the brother in whose home the church in Colosse gathers

Provocation: After greeting Philemon, his wife Apphia, and his son Archippus, Paul, "the aged" prisoner of Jesus Christ, informs Philemon that Onesimus is now a brother in the Lord. Because Onesimus has run away and stolen from his master (Philemon), Onesimus is subject to severe punishment. (Runaway slaves are branded with the letter "F" for fugitive and treated harshly.) Paul strongly hints to Philemon that he should forgive Onesimus, release him from his slavery, and send him back to Paul to help him in prison. Paul promises to pay back any money that Onesimus owes Philemon. Throughout the letter, Paul reminds Philemon that he led him (Philemon) to Christ, and therefore, Philemon owes him his life. Paul is confident that he will be released from prison. So he requests that Philemon prepare a room for him when he is able to visit the church.

Stop and read Philemon

PAUL WRITES EPHESIANS

Year: A.D. 61

From: Rome

To: A circuit letter to the churches in Asia Minor, particularly those in the Lycus Valley (which are about 4 years old). The earliest manuscripts omit the words "in Ephesus" and there are no personal greetings throughout the entire epistle.

Provocation: This letter is the crown of Paul's ministry, "the Divinest composition of man," and "the high water mark of Holy Writ." While the theme of Colossians is Christ the Head, the theme of Ephesians is Christ the Body. Ephesians is a matchless presentation of God's eternal purpose and the unsearchable riches the Christians have inherited in Christ. Paul begins by disclosing the church's wealth as it is *seated* with Christ in the heavenly places (chapters 1-3), he goes on to exhort the church in its *walk* in this world (chapters 4-5), and he ends by discussing the church's warfare as it *stands* against the enemy (chapter 6).

Stop and read Ephesians

Luke leaves Rome and travels to Philippi, where he stays with the church.[24] Titus travels to the Island of Crete and plants a number of churches there.

Spring 62
Crisis in Philippi

After some time, Paul decides to address the problems in Philippi that Epaphras reported to him. The problems are as follows:

- There are contentions, grumblings, and disputings present that are rooted in pride and petty jealousies. Two sisters in particular, Euodia and Syntyche, are quarreling with each other fiercely. (These women, along with Clement, have helped Paul labor in the gospel every time he was present in Philippi.)
- The Philippians are receiving persecution at the hands of their pagan neighbors who are libertines noted for their loose living and bondage to their fleshly appetites.
- The Philippians are also being agitated by Jewish missionaries who are urging them to be circumcised and come under the Law.
- Epaphras recovers from his illness, and Paul sends him to Philippi. Paul plans to send Timothy to Philippi once he learns about the results of his upcoming trial. He wants Timothy to bring back a report on the church's progress. Paul is optimistic that he will be released and plans to visit the church when that time comes. Philippians is Paul's last letter to a church that is recorded in the NT.[25]

PAUL WRITES PHILIPPIANS

Year: Spring 62
From: Rome
To: The church in Philippi (which is about 12 years old)
Provocation: Paul wants the Philippians to know how he is doing in Rome. He gives them an update on Epaphras (also called Epaphroditus) and tells them that he is sending him back to them. Paul encourages the church in the face of opposition. He addresses their contentions by presenting Christ—His humility and His lack of self-preservation. Paul puts the church on guard against the Judaizers

("the mutilation party" as he calls them) and against the pagan libertines. He tells the Philippians of his plan to send Timothy to them when he has a better idea of his own future. That future includes his desire to visit them when he is released from prison. Paul speaks directly to Luke and asks him to help two sisters in the church to reconcile and live in harmony (chapter 4:3). He ends the letter by thanking the church for its gracious financial gift. A highlight of this letter is found in chapter 2:6-11 where Paul quotes an ancient Christian hymn regarding the incarnation of Jesus Christ.

Stop and read Philippians

James (The Lord's Half-Brother) Is Martyred

Porcius Festus dies in office. Albinus is slated to replace Festus. But it will take at least five weeks for the news to travel from Judea to Rome and at least five more weeks for Albinus to travel from Rome to Judea. During this three-month waiting period, Ananus[26] the high priest convenes the Sanhedrin and brings "James the Just" (the half-brother of Jesus) and some others in Jerusalem before the council. Before the Sanhedrin, Ananus accuses James of blaspheming the Law. James is brought to the pinnacle of the temple, thrown down, and is clubbed and stoned to death.

Since James was held in high regard in Jerusalem as being a "Torah-true Jew," the fair-minded Jews in the city are offended by his execution. Albinus takes office, and Ananus is deposed for illegally convening the Sanhedrin.[27]

ENDNOTES

1. According to the Roman historian Tacitus (A.D. 117), Felix practiced every kind of cruelty and lust and wielded his power like a king with all the instincts of a slave.

2. Acts 23:33–24:27.

3. Acts 25–26.

4. The other seven apostolic workers probably returned to their homes after Paul was seized in Jerusalem.

5. According to the Western Text, the voyage from Caesarea to Myra took fifteen days.

6. I have intentionally omitted the details of the shipwreck. Luke's description of the shipwreck is a classic in ancient literature. It is a masterpiece of vivid narrative. A good deal of our knowledge of ancient seamanship comes from this account. Therefore, I would recommend that you read his firsthand account in Acts 27:14-44.

7. Acts 27.

8. Acts 28:1-11.

9. Philippians 1:13.

10. Acts 28:12-29.

11. Acts 28:30-31.

12. Philippians 1:12-18.

13. Ancient prisons did not provide meals or do laundry, so this was typically done by the prisoners' friends.

14. Colossians 4:10,14.

15. Ephesians 6:21; Colossians 4:7.

16. Colossians 1:1; Philippians 1:1; 2:19.

17. Colossians 4:14; Philemon 24.

18. Philemon 24; Colossians 4:10.

19. Epaphroditus seems to be the same person known as Epaphras. See John L. McKenzie, S.J., *Dictionary of the Bible* (Macmillan Publishing, 1965), p. 239; Matthew Henry's *Commentary on the Whole Bible: Introduction to the Epistle to the Colossians*). Both Epaphroditus (Philippians 2:25; 4:18) and Epaphras (Philemon 23; Colossians 1:7; 4:12) were coworkers with Paul and both were with Paul during the same Roman imprisonment. Epaphras planted churches, and Paul calls Epaphroditus an *apostolos* (Philippians 2:25). This all suggests that they were one person. Further, the name occurs very frequently in inscriptions in both Latin and Greek, whether in the full length "Epaphroditus," or in its contracted form "Epaphras" (Lightfoot, *Philippians*, 123).

20. Philemon 1-2.

21. Colossians 4:7; Ephesians 6:21.

22. This scenario is derived from mirror-reading Paul's words in Colossians and Philemon.

23. Colossians 4:9. According to tradition, Onesimus became an elder in the church of Ephesus. Thus Philemon undoubtedly freed him. If he had not, the letter of Philemon would no longer exist.

24. When Paul writes to the church in Philippi, he addresses someone he calls "true yokefellow" (Philippians 4:3). Many scholars believe this is a reference to Luke.

25. This scenario is derived from mirror-reading Paul's words in Philippians.

26. Ananus is also called Annas. He is the son of the high priest that bears the same name who is mentioned in the gospel story (John 18:13,24).

27. This account comes from the Jewish historian Josephus and the church historian Eusebius.

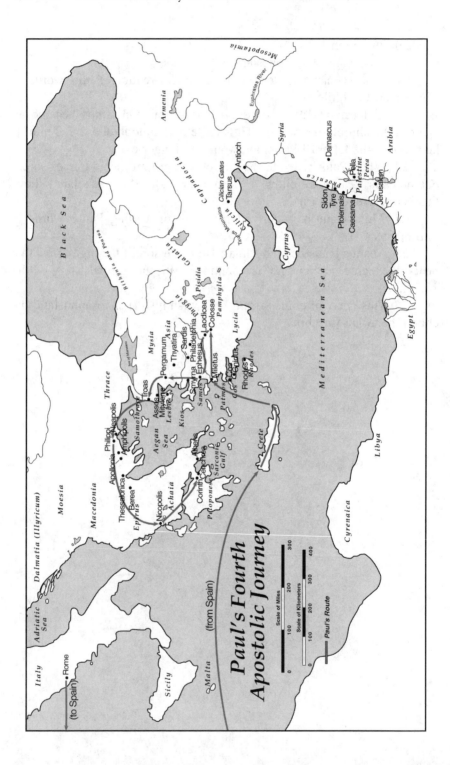

Paul's Fourth
Apostolic Journey

CHAPTER 13

THE POST-CAPTIVITY CHRONICLE

A.D. 63–A.D. 70

For I am already being poured out as a drink offering, and the time for my departure is close. I have fought the good fight, I have finished the race, I have kept the faith. In the future, there is reserved for me the crown of righteousness, which the Lord, the righteous Judge, will give me on that day, and not only to me, but to all those who have loved His appearing (2 Timothy 4:6-8).

PREVIEW OF PAUL'S FOURTH APOSTOLIC JOURNEY

Time: 2 years
Years: A.D. 63–65
Miles Traveled: Unknown
Churches Planted: (2) Nicopolis and Miletus
Time planted:
Nicopolis = Unknown
Miletus = Unknown

Peter and Silas have been spending time traveling in northwest Asia bordering the Black Sea (modern Turkey)—specifically the regions of Pontus, North Galatia, Cappadocia, and Bithynia where there are churches mixed with Jewish and Gentile believers.[1] Peter and Silas now come to Rome where they join John Mark.[2]

A.D. 63

After spending two years of house arrest in Rome, Paul is released for lack of evidence to convict him. Upon his release, Paul makes his long-awaited trip to Spain.[3] The visit is brief and no churches are planted.[4]

Paul travels southeast and meets Titus on the Island of Crete. Both men minister to the churches on the island. The churches are undergoing an assault of false teaching. As a result, they are falling apart. Paul leaves Titus on the island to strengthen the churches and to select overseers (elders) who will be able to care for the church when Titus leaves.

Paul travels northeast and spends some time in Asia Minor. He visits Miletus where he begins preaching the gospel. Paul sends a message to Trophimus in Ephesus to meet him in Miletus to help with the work. Trophimus joins him and a church is planted in Miletus—a community who expresses Jesus Christ. Regrettably, Trophimus gets sick. Paul heads off to Colosse as he had promised,[5] but he leaves Trophimus behind in Miletus.[6]

Timothy sends word to Paul in Colosse that the Ephesian church is being ravaged by false teachers. Paul meets Timothy in Ephesus and excommunicates two men from the church, Hymenaeus and Alexander. These men are blaspheming and teaching that the resurrection has already passed. They will not repent, so Paul has no other choice but to put them out of the church because they are damaging the faith of some of the believers.[7] Alexander, who is a metal-worker, retaliates by opposing Paul's message and causing him great harm.[8] A brother in the church in Ephesus named Onesiphorus is of great help to Paul.[9]

Paul leaves Timothy in Ephesus and instructs him to combat the false teachers in the church who are ambitious to teach the Law (yet know little about it). These men are teaching myths that pervert the creation account and they are debating over genealogies.[10] Paul heads off to Macedonia.

On his way to Macedonia, Paul visits the church in Troas and stays in the home of Carpus. Paul departs Troas, but he leaves behind his winter coat, some scrolls, and some parchments at Carpus' home.[11] Paul arrives in Macedonia and visits the church in Philippi as he had planned to do while in prison.[12]

Crisis in Ephesus

Despite Timothy's attempt to re-center the church of Ephesus back on Christ, the problems worsen. Paul's warning to the elders in Ephesus is finally coming to pass. Five years earlier he forewarned the Ephesian elders that wolves would penetrate the church and draw disciples after themselves with perverse teachings.[13]

The wolves have appeared in Ephesus.[14] The heresy they are teaching is a kind of Jewish proto-gnosticism. (Gnosticism will make its appearance in the second century. According to gnosticism, full salvation comes through special knowledge—*gnosis*—that only the initiated possess. In Ephesus, an embryonic form of the heresy has emerged.)[15] Here is what they are teaching:

- It is a sin to eat meat and to engage in marriage.[16]
- Eve is both a mediator and redeemer figure who pre-existed Adam.[17]
- Man came into existence because of a woman, and he was given enlightenment through the woman. Since Eve was the first to take a bite from the Tree of Knowledge, she is the bearer of special spiritual knowledge (called *gnosis*).[18]
- Women are called to lead people to the illuminating *gnosis* which was represented by the Tree of Knowledge. Redemption completely reversed the effects of the Fall so that men are no longer subject to earthly authorities and women are no longer subject to their husbands.[19]

Those in the Ephesian church who are accepting this heresy prefer the leadership of women over men. Male teachers were the first to spread the false doctrine in Ephesus.[20] But it finds fertile ground among the women in the church.[21]

The homes of the Ephesian women provide a network by which the heresy is spread rapidly through "gossip."[22] Some of the women are teaching the heresy in the church meetings and are lording it over (dominating) the men. They have also accepted the ideals of the "new women" of the Roman Empire. They are dressing in an immodest and exploitive way (like that of prostitutes) and are defying other accepted norms regarding marriage and family.[23]

There is also a problem with respect to how the widows are being cared for in the church.[24] Some of the widows have adopted the heresy, and others have family members who are able to care for them. Still worse, some of the younger widows who decided not to remarry are acting promiscuously.

Consequently, Timothy wants to know which widows the church ought to be responsible for. Further, some of the rich brethren in the church are trusting in their riches and are influencing their poorer brethren to desire wealth.

The church in Ephesus is in crisis and Timothy writes Paul about it. Upon hearing the news, Paul wishes to return to Ephesus. But he cannot. So he responds to Timothy by letter.[25]

PAUL WRITES 1 TIMOTHY

Year: A.D. 63

From: Philippi in Macedonia

To: Timothy who is in Ephesus

Provocation: In this letter, Paul reminds Timothy how the believers ought to behave themselves in the community (3:15). He encourages Timothy to be faithful to his ministry, and exhorts him to combat the proto-gnostic heresy that is spreading like a cancer in Ephesus. Paul gives Timothy practical instructions on how to do it. One solution is to forbid the women who are peddling the false doctrine from teaching in the meetings. He also addresses the problem of the Ephesian women accepting the ideals of the "new women" in their dress (2:9ff). Paul calls for the need to select new overseers (3:1ff) and exhorts the church to give respect to those overseers who are serving well (5:17ff). He exposes the spirit behind the present heresy and predicts that it will increase in the future (4:1ff). Paul exhorts Timothy to let no one despise his youth, but rather, to boldly proclaim the truth in the face of error. He also gives Timothy instructions on caring for the widows (5:1ff). Paul closes the letter by admonishing the contentious and the rich (6:3ff). Luke is with Paul and serves as his amanuensis to pen the letter. This letter, along with Titus and 2 Timothy, are written to Paul's coworkers rather than to a church. This fact, along with Luke's penmanship, account for the uniqueness of vocabulary and style in the so-called "Pastoral Epistles." (Labeling 1 Timothy, 2 Timothy, and Titus the "Pastoral Epistles" or the "Pastorals" is a misnomer. These letters were not given this label until the 18th century. Timothy and Titus were not pastors. They were apostolic workers.) While Paul was responsible for the content, Luke shaped the vocabulary and style.

Stop and read 1 Timothy

LUKE WRITES ACTS

Year: A.D. 63

From: Macedonia

To: Theophilus and the Gentiles

Provocation: Acts is an orderly account of the rise and progress of Christianity in its first thirty years. It is not a biography of Paul. Luke writes Acts to legitimize the early Christian movement (refuting the current objections to it) and to show how it spread to Rome. For this reason, Acts ends when Paul arrives in the Eternal City. Luke also shows how Christianity is the fulfillment of Judaism and is entitled to share in the liberty which the Empire accords to Judaism. Luke also writes for the edification of the churches. Acts is the second volume of his two-part work (Luke-Acts) describing the historicity of the Christian faith.

Timothy gets into trouble with the authorities in Ephesus, and he is put in jail.[26]

A Fire Burns in Rome
July 19, 64

A great fire rages for nine days, destroying ten out of the fourteen quarters of Rome. Shops, homes, and temples are destroyed in the heart of the city. Emperor Nero is blamed, so he looks for a scapegoat to deflect attention from himself. Since they are despised throughout the city, the Christians are blamed by Nero who says they burned the city to fulfill their prophecies.

The Roman Christians are immediately viewed as outcasts by the Roman citizens and are harassed because of it. Though they have not yet shed blood for their faith, the oppression is increasing. Some of the Jewish Christians begin re-attending the synagogue in order to circumvent the persecution.[27] They are returning to the Law, for it is safer to do so.[28] Timothy is released from jail.[29]

HEBREWS IS WRITTEN

Year: A.D. 64

From: Unknown, probably Apollos, Barnabas, or Silas

To: The Grecian (Hellenistic) Jewish believers in Rome

Provocation: The writer encourages the Jewish believers in their persecution and argues that they cannot have one foot in the Jewish camp and one foot in Christ's camp. His exhortation is to "let us go to Him outside the camp, bearing His reproach." The Book contains five parenthetical warnings against apostasy—i.e., leaving

Christ and returning back to sin and the Law (2:1-4; 3:7–4:13; 5:11–6:20; 10:26-39; 12:15-29). The beautiful theme that runs consistently throughout the entire letter is the High Priestly ministry of Jesus Christ. Jesus Christ is the supreme and only effective Mediator between God and man. He is the Author of a New Covenant which is far superior to the Old Covenant. The New Covenant is a "better" covenant that brings forth a "better" hope, "better" promises, and a "better" sacrifice in a "more perfect" tabernacle. The writer ends the letter by expressing his desire to see the church and sends greetings from those Italian Christians who are presently with the author outside of Italy.

Stop and read Hebrews

The Neronian Persecution
Spring 65

Nero's massacre of the Christians begins. Over the next three years, Nero will brutalize the Christians in such unspeakable ways that the Romans themselves have sympathy for them. He will have some sewn up in the skins of wild beasts to be preyed upon by dogs until they expire. Others he will dress up in shirts of stiff wax, fix them to the trees in his garden, and light them up as human torches.[30] The church in Rome has dwindled due to the killings. Priscilla and Aquila move to Ephesus to help Timothy care for the church. The persecution of the Christians spreads throughout the entire Roman Empire and lasts until A.D. 68, when Nero is banished from Rome and commits suicide.

Crisis in Crete

Paul is still in Macedonia, and Apollos and a lawyer named Zenas visit him there. Paul gets word from Titus in Crete that the churches on the island are still in crisis. The influence of the false teachers is growing. They are spreading the same heresy that Timothy is combating in Ephesus. Some of them are also encouraging rebellion and an immoral lifestyle. (The Cretans as a culture are noted for lying, engaging in wild parties, and gluttony.)[31] A number of families are being disrupted as a result.

Specifically, both the old and young men in the church are being influenced by the old Cretan lifestyle and are not exercising self-control.

Some are rebelling against the local authorities. Some of the older women are engaging in slander and are abusing wine. Paul is burdened to write to Titus and give him further instructions on handling the crisis.[32]

PAUL WRITES TITUS

Year: A.D. 65

From: Macedonia

To: Titus who is in Crete

Provocation: Paul encourages Titus to strengthen the things that remain in the churches at Crete. He gives him practical instructions on selecting elders (1:5ff). Paul exhorts Titus on how to silence those who are spreading heresy in Crete and how to encourage and remind the believers with the truth that is in Christ (1:10–3:11). He closes the letter by asking Titus to meet him in Nicopolis for the winter and promises to send either Tychicus or Artemas to replace him in Crete. Paul sends the letter off with Apollos and Zenas the lawyer and asks Titus to care for their needs while they are in Crete. Luke scribes the letter.

Stop and read Titus

Apollos and Zenas travel to Crete and deliver Paul's letter to Titus. Paul travels to Nicopolis, Greece and spends the winter there.[33] He plants a church in Nicopolis—a community who reflects God's nature. Paul sends Tychicus to replace Titus in Crete.[34]

When Tychicus arrives, Titus joins Paul in Nicopolis and helps him found the new church. When winter is over, Paul and Titus head off to Corinth to check on the church there. They then head for Ephesus and ask Erastus to join them. Erastus, however, cannot go so he stays in Corinth.[35]

Paul's Second Roman Imprisonment

The Neronian persecution continues to spread beyond Rome. On his way to Ephesus, Paul is arrested and taken back to Rome where he is imprisoned again. Paul is not enjoying house arrest as he did in his first imprisonment. Rather, he is put in the Mamertine dungeon (Rome's state prison) awaiting trial.[36] Although he can receive visitors, it is very difficult to locate him.

An Ephesian believer named Onesiphorus hunts for Paul in Rome. He finally finds him and refreshes Paul in prison, not being ashamed of his imprisonment.[37] Also, Tychicus, Demas, Titus, and a man named Crescens find Paul and stay with him for a time.[38]

Noting that war is on the horizon, Jews from the churches in Palestine begin to migrate to the churches in Asia Minor. Among them are Philip and his four daughters who relocate to the church in Hierapolis.[39]

John the Apostle Moves to Ephesus

With Paul in prison, John the apostle comes to Ephesus and joins Timothy. John sends some of his coworkers to minister to the churches in Asia Minor. In one of these churches, a self-appointed demagogue named Diotrephes rejects John's ministry along with the men John has sent to help the church.

Diotrephes' lust to have first place in the church is so extreme that he accuses John with wicked words and excommunicates those brethren who desire to receive the workers whom John has sent.

The heresy that liberty is license to sin has crept into the churches in Asia Minor also. False prophets have risen up in the churches in Asia Minor and are spreading the heresy. These false prophets are "antichrists." They have left the churches and have undermined the foundations of the gospel of Jesus Christ. However, they are still in contact with the believers and are leading some of them astray with their deviant gospel. Here is what they are teaching:

- The material world of matter is evil. Therefore, the Divine Christ could not have come to the earth in human flesh. He rather came in spirit and only seemed to be touchable human flesh.[40]
- Jesus was not the Son of God.
- Since salvation means deliverance from the physical world, including the physical body, it does not matter how a person behaves in their bodies.
- Since sin is part of the material world, sin does not exist for the Christian. We (the false prophets) are sinless.
- We (the false prophets) have special insight from God's Spirit to see these deeper truths.

As a consequence of embracing this false gospel, some of the brethren are exhibiting hatred toward one another. Others are claiming that they have never sinned and that sin does not exist.[41] John is burdened to write a gospel that portrays the real Christ, and several letters that specifically deal with the crisis in Asia Minor.

JOHN WRITES HIS GOSPEL

Year: A.D. 65
From: Ephesus
To: Unknown
Provocation: John presents Jesus Christ as the Heavenly, Eternal, Divine Son of God. The Book also includes information about Christ's early Judean ministry that is absent from the Synoptic Gospels (Matthew, Mark, and Luke). John also pays special attention to the Feasts of Israel as he traces the Lord's life.

JOHN WRITES 1 JOHN

Year: A.D. 65
From: Ephesus
To: The churches in Asia Minor
Provocation: Christ is Life, Light, and Love, and He has come in the flesh and was seen, heard, and handled by John himself. John refutes the present heresy that has spread in Asia Minor at every point by revealing God's nature in Christ. The fruit of that nature is love for the brethren and the refusal to habitually practice sin. All Christians have received insight ("knowledge") from the Holy Spirit, and all have the anointing of the Spirit to teach them truth. John exhorts the fathers, the young men, and the children in the church to abide in Christ. He closes the letter by exhorting the believers to guard themselves against false conceptions of God ("idols").

Stop and read 1 John

JOHN WRITES 2 JOHN

Year: A.D. 65
From: Ephesus
To: An unnamed local church in Asia Minor

Provocation: John addresses the church as a woman ("the elect lady") and its members as her "children." The letter warns the church against receiving itinerant teachers who bring a false gospel. John exhorts the believers not to admit false teachers into the church (which meets in a home) nor greet them. He closes with a greeting from the believers in Ephesus. He describes them as the "children" of a "sister" church.

Stop and read 2 John

JOHN WRITES 3 JOHN

Year: A.D. 65
From: Ephesus
To: Gaius who is in Asia Minor
Provocation: John commends Gaius for receiving the apostolic workers that he (John) has sent. But he warns Gaius about Diotrephes who does not receive John nor any of the workers that he has sent. (Gaius is part of a nearby church to which Diotrephes belongs.) John praises Gaius for his hospitality and exhorts him to not imitate evil (that is, Diotrephes). He deplores Diotrephes for his overlordship and ambition. John sends the letter with Demetrius, one of his coworkers whom he commends highly.

Stop and read 3 John

Crisis in the Churches of Northwest Asia

The Christians throughout the Empire are suffering severe persecution. Peter has received word that the churches in northwest Asia are suffering massive attack. They are distressed and in great need of encouragement.

The persecution has become so bad that the Gentile Christians are being tempted to revert back to their past pagan lifestyles to lessen the heat. Some of the believers are rebelling against local authorities because of the mistreatment and slander they are receiving from them. There is conflict in the home; husbands and wives are bickering. In some of the churches, the elders are exercising too much control in their attempt to keep the believers faithful in the midst of the pressure.[42]

PETER WRITES 1 PETER

Year: A.D. 65

From: Rome

To: The churches in northwest Asia: Pontus, North Galatia, Cappadocia, and Bithynia.

Provocation: Peter encourages his Jewish and Gentile brethren in the midst of their suffering, which is being shared by their fellow Christians everywhere (5:9). He exhorts the Gentile brethren not to revert back to the lifestyle they lived as pagans. He exhorts the church to yield to their local authorities and gives practical instructions to family members about how to treat one another. Peter also charges the elders to lead by example rather than by force. Throughout the letter, Peter uses the general Greek word for suffer (*pascho*) twelve times—more than in any other NT letter. Given its excellent Greek style, the letter is scribed by Silas (Silvanus) who is with Peter in Rome. (Peter is a Galilean fisherman. While he no doubt could speak and write a little Greek for business purposes, his Greek writing skills are very limited.) Peter closes the letter by sending greetings from John Mark and the church in Rome. He calls Rome by its code-name "Babylon." Peter sends the letter with Silas who reads it to each of the churches.

Stop and read 1 Peter

War in Jerusalem
Spring 66

The Jewish revolt against Rome begins. For the next four years, war will rage between Jewish revolutionaries and Roman soldiers beginning in Judea and spreading throughout Palestine. There is great unrest and discord in the city of Jerusalem. The Christians leave the city and disperse into the Gentile churches outside of Palestine.

A.D. 67

Paul is still imprisoned in Rome. Priscilla and Aquila are still in Ephesus trying to save the church from the constant threat of heresy. The false teachers are winning out, and there is a wholesale departure from Paul's ministry in Asia Minor. Further, because Paul is imprisoned, the Christians no longer wish to associate with him out of fear that they too will be imprisoned.

Two brothers in Christ that Paul trusted named Phygelus and Hermogenes turn away from him. Demas forsakes Paul because of his love for the world and returns to Thessalonica. Paul sends a man named Crescens to Galatia and Titus to Dalmatia (Illyricum) to work with the churches there. He sends Tychicus and Onesiphorus back to Ephesus to help Priscilla and Aquila.

Paul's preliminary hearing (*primo actio*) occurs, but no one is present to support him.[43] Due to the lack of support for Paul, the trial goes forward. Upon hearing this, Luke immediately visits Paul in prison.[44] Some of the survivors from Nero's persecution of the Roman church also visit Paul to check on him from time to time. Among them are Eubulus, Pudens, Linus, and Claudia.

Paul is burdened for the future of the churches. He knows that his time of departure is near. Paul longs to see Timothy, and prays for him day and night. He wishes to encourage Timothy in his calling, to exhort him to be optimistic and strong in the face of his opposers, to warn him of the coming apostasy (falling away), and to remind him of those intangible things that he (Paul) has deposited in him over the years.

PAUL WRITES 2 TIMOTHY

Year: A.D. 67

From: Rome

To: Timothy who is in Ephesus

Provocation: Paul encourages and reminds Timothy about the perils and the duties of an apostolic worker. He exhorts Timothy to train men who are called, just as he (Paul) trained Timothy (2:2). He gives Timothy instructions on how to deal with those who have turned away from the truth, exhorts him on how to care for the church, encourages him to endure suffering, charges him to be faithful to his calling, and warns him about what lies in store for the future. Paul declares that he has run the Christian race well and that he is ready to be offered up to his Lord in death. He puts Timothy on guard against Alexander the metal-worker. Paul closes the letter by asking Timothy to visit him before winter. He requests that he bring John Mark along too. He asks for his winter cloak (indicating it is cold in the dungeon), his scrolls and parchments, all of which he left at Troas. Paul sends greetings to Priscilla and Aquila and the household of Onesiphorus. He sends greetings to Timothy from Eubulus, Pudens, Linus, Claudia and the rest of the church in Rome. Luke scribes the letter.

Stop and read 2 Timothy

Peter knows that his time on earth is also coming to an end. He is burdened to write one last letter to the churches in the Diaspora.[45] He has it on his heart to remind them of the things of Christ that have been deposited in them, to encourage them to continue to walk steadfastly in the Lord, and to warn them of coming false teachers.[46]

PETER WRITES 2 PETER

Year: A.D. 67

From: Rome

To: The churches in northwest Asia: Pontus, North Galatia, Cappadocia, and Bithynia.

Provocation: Peter reminds the churches of the true apostolic message which is being threatened. He also encourages the believers to cultivate their spiritual lives. Peter warns the church about the coming of false teachers and their destructive heresies, exposing their motives and teachings in detail. He also informs the churches that his time on this earth is coming to a close. Peter ends the letter by commending to them Paul's letters, which he calls "Scripture."

Stop and read 2 Peter

Paul and Peter Are Martyred
June 29, 67

According to early church tradition, this is the day that Paul is beheaded in Rome during Nero's reign.

Around the same time, Peter is found confounding the magic of Simon Magus, who is favored by Nero. Peter is imprisoned and leads a captain of the guard to Christ, along with many others. Peter is scourged, then crucified upside down because he does not feel worthy to die as did his Lord.[47]

Aristarchus from Thessalonica, Erastus from Corinth, Trophimus from Ephesus, Joseph Barsabbas from Jerusalem, and Ananias of Damascus, along with many other Christians, are all martyred under Nero's reign.[48]

A.D. 68

Andrew, the apostle and brother of Peter, is crucified in Patras, Greece on an x-shaped cross.[49] Luke is crucified with him.[50] After preaching the gospel in India, Armenia, Southern Arabia, and Ethiopia, Bartholomew (also called Nathanael) one of the Twelve, is beaten and crucified in Albanopolis, Armenia.[51]

John Mark brings the gospel to Alexandria, Egypt. While there, he enrages a mob by telling them that the pagan god, Serapis, is worthless. Mark is dragged with a rope around his neck through the streets by horses and then imprisoned for the night. The following morning, the same ordeal is repeated until his death.

Nero and Vespasian
June 9, 68

After fourteen years of Nero's reign, the Roman people can no longer tolerate their cruel and embarrassing emperor. So they revolt against Nero. The Senate declares him to be a public enemy of the State, and soldiers pursue him. Upon hearing this, Nero hides at the home of one of his freedmen in a villa outside of Rome where he commits suicide. His famous last words are: "What an artist the world is losing in me."

Crisis in the Churches of the Dispersion

False teachers have subtly infiltrated the dispersed Jewish churches and are spreading a false doctrine that perverts God's grace to be license to sin. These false brethren have successfully disguised themselves as true believers and have managed to partake of the Lord's Supper with the church.[52] These false teachers can be described as follows:

- They are distorting the gospel by advocating sexual license under the banner of God's grace.

- They are "dreamers," seeing visions that originate from themselves and not from the Lord.
- They slander angels, which means they despise the Law of Moses that was delivered by angels.
- They indulge their own needs when eating the Lord's Supper.
- They are grumblers and malcontents, pursuing their own will rather than God's.
- They are arrogant and use flattery to take advantage of God's people.
- They are scoffers, laughing at moral purity and Divine judgment.
- They are devoid of the Spirit of God and provoke divisions in the church.

Jude possesses a copy of Peter's second letter.[53] In it, he sees the fulfillment of Peter's prediction about the coming of false teachers coming to pass before his eyes.[54] Jude, the half-brother of Jesus and brother of "James the Just," is burdened about this problem.[55]

JUDE WRITES THE LETTER OF JUDE

Year: A.D. 68

From: Unknown

To: The dispersed Jewish Christians in and outside of Palestine

Provocation: Jude exposes and announces condemnation on the false teachers who have infiltrated the churches. He also reminds and exhorts the believers to return to and contend for the original faith that the apostles delivered to them.

Stop and read Jude

December 69

Vespasian is officially proclaimed Emperor of Rome.

A.D. 70

Vespasian is occupied in Alexandria. While he is away from Rome, he puts his elder son, Titus, in charge of military affairs. His younger son, Domitian, is given authority to act as Ceasar to the Empire.

Domitian exiles John, the apostle, to the Isle of Patmos for the testimony of Jesus Christ.[56] John is sentenced to labor in the mines of the island. (The Island of Patmos is eight miles long and five miles wide and sits 50 miles southwest of Ephesus.)

JOHN WRITES REVELATION

Year: A.D. 70

From: The Island of Patmos

To: Seven churches in Asia Minor

Provocation: On the Isle of Patmos, John is given a symbolic vision of Jesus Christ and the future purpose of God. The Lord Jesus tells John to write the vision down in a book and to send it to the seven churches in Asia Minor (1:10-11). Revelation encompasses the things that John has "seen, the things which are, and the things which shall take place after these things" (1:19).

The Roman Siege of Jerusalem
May-August 70

The population of Jerusalem is now 600,000. Titus, the son of Emperor Vespasian, marches into Jerusalem with his troops and overtakes the city. The Roman army breaches the first and second walls of Jerusalem. Mass execution of the escapees begins. There are up to 500 crucifixions per day outside the city.[57]

Famine begins within Jerusalem. As the famine takes its toll, some of the Jews resort to infanticide and cannibalism to survive. The Romans destroy the Tower of Antonia and are shocked at the conditions inside the city, including the cannibalism.

The Romans take the temple and the city. They enter the temple and set it afire by a reckless Roman torch. The temple is desecrated and utterly destroyed.[58] Remembering Jesus' warning in Luke 21:20-24, the Christians have already fled the city.[59] No less than one million perish in the seige and over 90,000 are led into captivity.

The Jerusalem church is dispersed again. The Jewish Christians are now forced to sit down and eat with their "unclean," Law-free Gentile brethren in the Gentile churches that Paul and his coworkers have planted all throughout the Roman Empire.[60]

The Church After A.D. 70

John, the apostle, is released from his banishment on the Island of Patmos. He moves back to Ephesus where he lives out the rest of his life. John dies of natural causes in A.D. 98 at the age of 100.

The apostasy that Paul and Peter prophecied about continues to flourish. Silas brings the gospel to the Island of Rhodes. He later moves to Northern Greece where he dies.[61] Philip, one of the Twelve apostles, has a powerful ministry in Carthage, North Africa. He then travels to Asia Minor where he converts the wife of a Roman governor (proconsul). In retaliation, the governor has Philip arrested and cruelly put to death.

Matthew (also called Levi), one of the Twelve, opens doors to the gospel in Persia, Egypt, and Ethiopia. He is killed with a spear in Nadabah, Ethiopia. Matthias, the apostle who replaced Judas Iscariot, preaches Christ in Asia Minor and Syria. He is burned to death in Syria.[62]

Thomas (also called Didymus), one of the Twelve, brings the gospel to Syria and India. He preaches to Parthians, Medes, and Persians. Thomas is stabbed to death by Brahman priests in Mylapore, India in A.D. 72. Barnabas is martyred in Salamis, Cyprus in A.D. 73.

Simon the Zealot and Judas (also called Thaddeus), two of the twelve apostles, bring the gospel to Great Britain. They then go to Persia to proclaim Christ where they are torn apart by a Persian mob in A.D. 79.[63] James, the apostle and son of Alphaeus, also preaches the gospel in Persia where he is beaten and stoned to death by the Jews at the age of 94.[64]

In A.D. 96, Titus dies on the Island of Crete. Timothy dies a year later in Ephesus. He is stoned to death after protesting the festivities in honor of the pagan goddess Diana (Artemis).

Following the death of the apostles and their coworkers, the light and glow of the first-century church begins to fade. Man-made systems and humanly-devised traditions slowly evolve to replace her glory and dim her light.[65] Yet God does not give up on His eternal purpose. Throughout the centuries, the Lord progressively works toward restoring her pristine simplicity and glory…until the time that she—the *ekklesia*—the community of the King—the Bride of Christ, has made herself ready for her Bridegroom.[66]

ENDNOTES

1. 1 Peter 1:1. The Lord did not allow Paul to minister in some of these regions (Acts 16:6-10). Pontus-Bithnyia formed a single province, but they are separated in 1 Peter 1:1 because Peter's list represents the travel route that he and Silas took when visiting these churches.

2. 1 Peter 5:12-13. Peter views John Mark as a son.

3. Romans 15:24-28. According to Clement of Rome (A.D. 96) and the Muritorian Canon (second century), Paul traveled to Spain after his release from his first Roman imprisonment.

4. By going to Spain, Paul fulfilled Christ's commission to him in Acts 13:47...he took the gospel to the "ends of the earth." Historically, no churches in Spain claimed Pauline origins so we assume that there was little fruit from the trip.

5. Philemon 22.

6. 2 Timothy 4:20.

7. 1 Timothy 1:20; 2 Timothy 2:17-18. Philetus was also teaching this heresy, but he probably left the church on his own.

8. 2 Timothy 4:14-15.

9. 2 Timothy 1:16-18.

10. 1 Timothy 1:3-7; 2 Timothy 4:4.

11. These scrolls may have been OT books, and the parchments were notebooks. They probably contained notes that Paul had used when he ministered in the various churches. They also may have been copies of previous letters he had written to the churches since it was the normal practice of the day to retain copies of letters that were dispatched.

12. Philippians 1:19,25; 1 Timothy 1:3.

13. Acts 20:28-30.

14. 1 Timothy 1:3-7; 6:3-5.

15. Paul refers to the heresy when he says to Timothy, "Turn away from godless chatter and the opposing ideas of what is falsely called gnosis"—1 Timothy 6:20.

16. 1 Timothy 4:1-3.

17. Paul refutes this concept in 1 Timothy 2:5,13-14.

18. The second-century gnostics taught this.

19. Paul refutes this concept in 1 Timothy 2:9-15.

20. 1 Timothy 1:20; 2 Timothy 2:17.

21. 1 Timothy 4:7; 2 Timothy 3:6-9.

22. 1 Timothy 3:11; 5:13-15.

23. Under ancient Roman law, you are what you wear. The way that wives dressed in public sent clear signals to men—signals that they were either modest or promiscuous women. As stated earlier, "the new women" of the Roman Empire were liberated married women who pursued their social lives at the expense of their families and who defied previously accepted norms of marriage fidelity and chastity. They were sexually promiscuous and dressed to seduce. Because Paul was a liberator of women, it is not difficult to see that some Christian women associated his views on a woman's freedom with the immoral ideals of the "new women." For a detailed discussion on how the women in Ephesus were being influenced by the ideals of the "new women," see Bruce Winter's *Roman Wives, Roman Widows: The Appearance of New Women and the Pauline Communities* (Eerdmans), Chapters 6–7.

24. Forty percent of women between the ages of 40 and 50 are widows. As a group, they comprise thirty percent of women in the ancient world. The Christian community in Ephesus decided that only women who were at least 60 years old should be supported by the church.

25. This scenario is derived from mirror-reading Paul's words in 1 Timothy.

26. Hebrews 13:23.

27. Fifteen years previous to this, the Jewish Christians in Rome had suffered public abuse and the confiscation of property when Claudius expelled them from the city in A.D. 49 (Hebrews 10:32-34).

28. Judaism is protected under Roman law, while Christianity is rapidly being seen as a sect that is separate from the Jewish faith.

29. This scenario is derived from mirror-reading Hebrews.

30. The Roman historian Tacitus describes the bloodbath graphically.

31. In his letter to Titus, Paul quotes the Cretan prophet Epimenides who says, "Cretans are always liars, evil beasts, lazy gluttons" (Titus 1:12).

32. This scenario is derived from mirror-reading Paul's words in Titus and 2 Timothy 4.

33. Because winter-time was unsafe for travel, both for sea and land, Paul always chose a place to winter (e.g., Corinth, Malta, Nicopolis). This also accounts for his urgent plea to Timothy to "do your best to come before winter" (2 Timothy 4:21).

34. Titus 3:12-13. Paul may have sent a man named Artemas instead of Tychicus.

35. 2 Timothy 4:20.

36. Paul spent as much as twenty-five percent of his apostolic ministry in prison.

37. The first-century Roman culture is dominated by honor and shame. There is a great stigma that goes with being imprisoned. The public exposure of being charged as a criminal is both degrading and lifelong. For Paul's shame concerns, see Philippians 1:12-20; 2 Timothy 1:8,11-12, 16; 2:9.

38. 2 Timothy 1:16; 4:10-12.

39. Their tombs were located in this town.

40. This denial of the Lord's incarnation later came to be known as *docetism*. Docetism is the belief that Christ could not possibly dwell in a human body. His body must have seemed (Greek *dokeo*) to be human.

41. This scenario is derived from mirror-reading John's words in 1 John, 2 John, and 3 John.

42. This scenario is derived from mirror-reading 1 Peter.

43. 2 Timothy 4:16.

44. This scenario is derived from mirror-reading Paul's words in 2 Timothy.

45. The Jews who are dispersed into Gentile nations.

46. This scenario is derived from mirror-reading Peter's words in 2 Peter.

47. This is the testimony of history. Jesus predicted the death that Peter would die (see John 21:18-19).

48. This account is based on church tradition.

49. The following accounts are based on church tradition.

50. Another tradition says that Luke died of natural causes in Boeotia at the age of 84.

51. One tradition says that he was flayed alive by a whip and then crucified head downward.

52. Jude describes the Lord's Supper as the "love (*agape*) feast" (Jude 12).

53. Probably given to him by Silas.

54. Peter predicted the coming of false teachers in 2 Peter 2:1ff. Jude refers to this prophecy in Jude 17ff (compare Jude 17-18 with 2 Peter 3:3). When speaking about the false teachers, Jude draws heavily from Peter's second letter (compare Jude 4-18 with 2 Peter 2:1–3:3).

55. This scenario is derived from mirror-reading Jude's words in Jude.

56. Because church tradition says that Domitian exiled John to the Island of Patmos, many scholars have dated the Book of Revelation to be

during Domitian's reign as Roman Emperor in the 90s. However, Domitian served temporarily as Emperor in A.D. 70 when his father was away from Rome. The weight of internal evidence in the Book of Revelation suggests that it was written before the destruction of Jerusalem (see John A.T. Robinson's *Redating the New Testament*, Westminster Press, Chapter 8 for details). The little known fact of Domitian's temporary reign meshes the internal evidence with the testimony of church history quite nicely.

57. According to Josephus, the Romans chopped down so many trees to make crosses that they completely stripped the hills of Jerusalem of the woods that covered them.

58. This account comes from the Jewish historian Josephus.

59. Eusebius, the church historian, wrote how the Christians were supernaturally warned by the Lord to flee Jerusalem before the bloodbath began. Many of them moved to the Greek city of Pella in the region of Perea, east of the Jordan River (the Transjordan).

60. A few stubborn ones founded the Ebionite heresy, which rejected Paul's writings, the virgin birth, Christ's Divinity, and espoused that all followers of Jesus must follow the Law of Moses.

61. These accounts are based on church tradition.

62. Other traditions say he was stoned to death and beheaded in Jerusalem by the Jews, he was killed with a lance or axe by the Jews, or he was crucified by the Romans.

63. One tradition says that Simon was martyred in Great Britain in A.D. 74.

64. Another tradition says James was crucified.

65. See my book *Pagan Christianity* for the story of how the church embraced man-made traditions, baptized them, and adopted them into the Christian faith.

66. For an introduction to the story of God's restoration work throughout the ages, see John Kennedy's *The Torch of the Testimony* (SeedSowers), E.H. Broadbent's *The Pilgrim Church* (Pickering & Inglis), and Charles Schmitt's *Floods Upon Dry Ground* (Destiny Image).

CHAPTER 14

THE FOURTH MOTION: THE SON RETURNS TO EARTH

The seventh angel blew his trumpet, and there were loud voices in heaven saying: The kingdom of the world has become the kingdom of our Lord and of His Messiah, and He will reign forever and ever! (Revelation 11:15).

He did this to present the church to Himself in splendor, without spot or wrinkle or any such thing, but holy and blameless (Ephesians 5:27).

He made known to us the mystery of His will, according to His good pleasure that He planned in Him for the administration of the days of fulfillment—to bring everything together in the Messiah, both things in heaven and things on earth in Him (Ephesians 1:9-10).

And He [the Father] *shall send Jesus Christ, which before was preached unto you: Whom the heavens must receive until the times of restitution of all things, which God has spoken by the mouth of His holy prophets since the world began* (Acts 3:20-21).

Then comes the end, when He hands over the kingdom to God the Father, when He abolishes all rule and all authority and power. For He must reign until He puts all His enemies under His feet. The last enemy He abolishes is death (1 Corinthians 15:24-26).

The appointed hour has come. The Son of God returns to earth to take His beloved Bride...for she has made herself ready. The Son presents His Bride to Himself and then to His Father. The Son establishes His

Kingdom on earth and reigns over all things. He puts all things under His feet—even death, which is the last enemy. The Son reconciles the universe to Himself and brings all things together into subjection to His Lordship. Jesus Christ is now King of kings and Lord of lords, possessor of Heaven and earth. He is preeminent over all things. The Son then hands everything that has been summed up into Himself back to His Father.

The story continues in the timeless future...

CHAPTER 15

THE FINAL MOTION:
THE GODHEAD IN ETERNITY FUTURE

*Then I saw a new heaven and a new earth, for the first heaven
and the first earth had passed away, and the sea existed no
longer. I also saw the Holy City, new Jerusalem, coming down
out of heaven from God, prepared like a bride adorned for her
husband. Then I heard a loud voice from the throne: Look! God's
dwelling is with men, and He will live with them. They will be His
people, and God Himself will be with them and be their
God...Then one of the seven angels, who had held the seven
bowls filled with the seven last plagues, came and spoke with
me: "Come, I will show you the bride, the wife of the Lamb"*
(Revelation 21:1-3,9).

*For He has put everything under His feet. But when it says
"everything" is put under Him, it is obvious that He who puts
everything under Him is the exception. And when everything is
subject to Him, then the Son Himself will also be subject to Him
who subjected everything to Him, so that God may be all in all*
(1 Corinthians 15:27-28).

S pace and time are no more. Nothing exists except the Trinitarian
Community: God the Father, God the Son, and God the Holy Spirit.
There is also a new person added. A Woman. The Bride. And she is made
up of the community of the redeemed. The Son takes His Bride into mar-
ital union, and the *Bride*—a virgin—becomes the *Wife* of the Lamb.

This Woman was hidden in the Son in eternity past. But now, in eternity future, she is fully manifested and brought into union with God. This

Woman is the church. She is the mystery that has been hidden in God from the foundation of the world. And you, dear Christian, are part of her!

The three Persons of the Divine community consummate their plan of expanding their fellowship—Jesus Christ and His Wife experience one-ness with the Godhead. The Son returns all things He has inherited to His Father, and God becomes *All* in *All*.

EPILOGUE

The story that you have just read is the untold saga of God's eternal purpose. It is the story of Jesus Christ and His magnificent counterpart—the *ekklesia*—the church—that spiritual community who reflects the community of the Godhead.

The NT contains the drama of her Lord's life on earth, her conception, her birth, the formative years of her life on earth, and her destiny. She, along with her Bridegroom, the Lord Jesus Christ, is God's central and consuming thought. He…and she…are what your NT is all about.

And because you are part of her—that heavenly community—the Bride of Jesus Christ…this story is *your* story!

BIBLIOGRAPHY

T his informal bibliography makes no pretense at being exhaustive. It merely attempts to supply the reader with the source materials used in this book. Commonly debated subjects like the North Galatian vs. South Galatian hypothesis, the theory that Paul experienced an Ephesian imprisonment, and scholarly disputes over NT chronology, the date, provenance, and authorship of each NT Book are treated in many of these volumes.

God's Central Goal of Establishing Communities That Display His Nature
Austin-Sparks, T. *The Stewardship of the Mystery: Volumes 1 & 2*, Testimony Book Ministry.
Giles, Kevin. *What on Earth is the Church? An Exploration in New Testament Theology*, InterVarsity Press.
Grenz, Stanley. *Theology for the Community of God*, Eerdmans.
Lohfink, Gerhard. *Jesus and Community*, Fortress Press.
Miller, Hal. *Christian Community: Biblical or Optional?*, Servant Books.
Nee, Watchman. *The Glorious Church,* Living Stream Ministry.
    The Mystery of Christ, Living Stream Ministry.
Snyder, Howard. *The Community of the King*, InterVarsity Press.

Paul's Life and Ministry
Ball, Charles Ferguson. *The Life and Times of the Apostle Paul*, Tyndale.
Bornkamm, Gunther. *Paul*, Harper and Row.
Bruce, F.F. *In the Steps of the Apostle Paul*, Kregel.
    Jesus and Paul: Places They Knew, Thomas Nelson.
    Paul: Apostle of the Heart Set Free, Eerdmans.
    The Pauline Circle, Paternoster Press.
Coneybeare, W.J. and J.S. Howson. *The Life and Epistles of St. Paul*, Eerdmans.
Galli, Mark, ed. *Paul and His Times: Christian History Magazine*, Christianity Today Publishers.
Glover, T.R. *Paul of Tarsus*, Hendrickson.

Grant, Michael. *Paul in the Roman World: The Conflict at Corinth*, Westminster Press.

Hawthorne, Gerald F., Ralph P. Martin, Daniel G. Reid, eds. *Dictionary of Paul and His Letters*, InterVarsity Press.

Hengel, Martin. *Paul Between Damascus and Antioch: The Unknown Years*, John Knox Press.

Meinardus, Otto F.A. *St. Paul in Ephesus and the Cities of Galatia and Cyprus*, Lycabettus Press.

    St. Paul in Greece, Lycabettus Press.

    St. Paul's Last Journey, Melissa Media (or Caratzas Brothers Publishing).

    St. John of Patmos and the Seven Churches of the Apocalypse, Lycabettus Press.

Marshall, David. *Footprints of Paul*, Autumn House.

Murphy-O'Connor, Jerome. *Paul: A Critical Life*, Clarendon Press.

    Paul the Letter-Writer: His World, His Options, His Skills, The Liturgical Press.

Pollock, John. *The Man Who Shook the World*, Victor Books.

Porter, Stanley E. *Paul in Acts*, Hendrickson.

Rainer, Riesner. *Paul's Early Period: Chronology, Mission Strategy, Theology*, Eerdmans.

Ramsey, W.M. *St. Paul the Traveler and Roman Citizen*, Hodder and Stoughton.

Smith, David. *Life and Letters of St. Paul*, Harper Brothers.

White, Jefferson. *Evidence & Paul's Journeys*. Parsagard Press.

Winter, Bruce. *When Paul Left Corinth: The Influence of Secular Ethics and Social Change*, Eerdmans.

Witherington, Ben. *The Paul Quest: The Renewed Search for the Jew of Tarsus*, InterVarsity Press.

Worth, Roland H. *The Seven Cities of the Apocalypse and Greco-Asian Culture*, Paulist Press.

The Acts Narrative

Bruce, F.F. *The Acts of the Apostles: Greek Text with Introduction and Commentary*, Wipf & Stock.

    The Book of the Acts (Revised, 1988 Edition), Eerdmans.

Hemer, Colin J. *The Book of Acts in the Setting of Hellenistic History*, J.C.B. Mohr.

Guthrie, Donald. *The Apostles*, Zondervan.

Marshall, I. Howard. *The Acts of the Apostles*, InterVarsity Press.

Scroggie, W. Graham. *The Unfolding Drama of Redemption: Volume 2*, Kregel.

Wenham, David and Steve Walton. *Exploring the New Testament: A Guide to the Gospels and Acts*, Society for Promoting Christian Knowledge.

Winter, Bruce, ed. *The Book of Acts in Its First Century Setting (6 Volumes)*, Eerdmans.

    Volume 1: *The Book of Acts in Its Ancient Literary Setting*, Eerdmans.

Volume 2: *The Book of Acts in Its Graeco-Roman Setting*, Eerdmans.

Volume 3: *The Book of Acts and Paul in Roman Custody*, Eerdmans.

Volume 4: *The Book of Acts in Its Palestinian Setting*, Eerdmans.

Volume 5: *The Book of Acts in Its Diaspora Setting*, Eerdmans.

Volume 6: *The Book of Acts in Its Theological Setting*, Eerdmans.

Witherington, Ben. *The Acts of the Apostles: A Socio-Rhetorical Commentary*, Eerdmans.

The New Testament Epistles

Bruce, F.F. *The Epistles of John*, Eerdmans.

Guthrie, Donald. *New Testament Introduction*, InterVarsity Press.

Marshall, I. Howard, Steven Travis, & Ian Paul. *Exploring the New Testament: A Guide to the Letters & Revelation*, InterVarsity Press.

New Century Bible (New Testament Series), Oliphants.

New International Biblical Commentary (New Testament Series), Hendrickson.

Roetzel, Calvin. *The Letters of Paul: Conversations in Context*, Westminster John Knox Press.

The New International Commentary of the New Testament, Eerdmans.

The New International Greek Testament Commentary, Eerdmans.

The Tyndale New Testament Commentaries, InterVarsity Press.

Witherington, Ben. *Grace in Galatia: A Commentary on Paul's Letter to the Galatians*, Eerdmans.

Conflict & Community in Corinth: A Socio-Rhetorical Commentary on 1 and 2 Corinthians, Eerdmans.

Paul's Letter to the Romans: A Socio-Rhetorical Commentary, Eerdmans.

Revelation, The New Cambridge Bible Commentary.

Word Biblical Commentary (New Testament Portion), Word Books.

Life in the Roman Empire

Blaiklock, E.M. *Cities of the New Testament*, Fleming Revell.

Casson, Lionel. *Everyday Life in Ancient Rome*, John Hopkins University Press.

Travel in the Ancient World, John Hopkins University Press.

Corbishley, Mike. *What Do We Know About the Romans?*, Peter Bedrick Books.

Cornell, Tim and John Matthews. *Atlas of the Roman World*, Facts on File, Inc.

Durant, Will. *Caesar and Christ*, Simon and Schuster.

Harris, William. *Ancient Literacy*, Harvard University Press.

Goodenough, Simon. *Citizens of Rome*, Crown Publishers.

King, Marie Gentert, ed. *Foxe's Book of Martyrs*, Spire Books.

Lampe, Peter. *From Paul to Valentinus: Christians at Rome in the First Two Centuries*, Fortress.

Liversidge, Joan. *Everyday Life in the Roman Empire*, G.P. Putnam's Sons.

Macaulay, David. City: *A Story of Roman Planning and Construction*, Houghton Mifflin Co.

Marks, A.J. and G.I.F. Tingay. *The Romans*, EDC Publishing.

Ramsey, W.M. *The Church in the Roman Empire*, G.P. Putnam's Sons.
Rhoads, David M. *Israel in Revolution 6-74 C.E.*, Fortress Press.
Saller, Richard. *The Roman Empire: Economy, Society, and Culture*, Berkeley.
Smallwood, E. Mary. *The Jews Under Roman Rule*, Leiden.
Winter, Bruce. *Roman Wives, Roman Widows: The Appearance of New Women and the Pauline Communities*, Eerdmans.
Seeking the Welfare of the City: Christians as Benefactors and Citizens, Eerdmans.

The Social, Cultural, and Political Background of the New Testament Church

Barr, David. *An Introduction: New Testament Story*, Wadsworth Publishing Company.
Bruce, F.F. *New Testament History*, Doubleday.
Peter, Stephen, James & John: Studies in Non-Pauline Christianity, Eerdmans.
Evans, Craig and Stanley Porter, eds. *Dictionary of New Testament Background*, InterVarsity Press.
Ferguson, Everett. *Backgrounds of Early Christianity*, Eerdmans.
Jeffers, James. *The Greco-Roman World of the New Testament Era: Exploring the Background of Early Christianity*, InterVarsity Press.
Judge, E.A. *The Social Pattern of Christian Groups in the First Century*, Tyndale Press.
Malherbe, Abraham J. *Social Aspects of Early Christianity*, Fortress Press.
Martin, Ralph P. and Peter Davids, eds. *Dictionary of the Later New Testament & Its Development*, InterVarsity Press.
Meeks, Wayne. *The First Urban Christians: The Social World of the Apostle Paul*, Yale University Press.
The Moral World of the First Christians, John Knox Press.
Miller, Wayne D. *New Testament Churches*, Miller Publications.
Stambaugh, John E. and David L. Balch. *The New Testament in Its Social Environment*, The Westminster Press.
Stark, Rodney. *The Rise of Christianity: A Sociologist Reconsiders History*, Princeton University Press.
Stowers, Stanley. *Letter Writing in Greco-Roman Antiquity*, John Knox Press.
Theissen, Gerd. *Social Reality and the Early Christians: Theology, Ethics, and the World of the New Testament*, Fortress Press.
Tidball, Derek. *The Social Context of the New Testament: Sociological Analysis*, Zondervan.
Witherington, Ben. *New Testament History: A Narrative Account*, Baker Books.

The Chronology of the First-Century Church

Barker, Kenneth, ed. "Timeline of Paul's Life," *The NIV Study Bible*, Zondervan.
Bruce, F.F. *Chronological Questions in the Acts of the Apostles*, J. Rylands.
Finegan, Jack. *Handbook of Biblical Chronology*, Princeton University Press.

Gunther, John J. Paul: *Messenger and Exile: A Study in the Chronology of His Life and Letters*, Judson Press.

Hoehner, Harold. "A Chronological Table of the Apostolic Age," *Chronological and Background Charts to the New Testament*, ed. H. Wayne House, Zondervan.

Chronological Aspects of the Life of Christ, Zondervan.

"New Testament Chronology," *Nelson's Illustrated Bible Dictionary*, Nelson.

Jewett, Robert. *A Chronology of Paul's Life*, Fortress Press.

Ludemann, Gerd. *Paul, Apostle to the Gentiles: Studies in Chronology*, Fortress.

Ogg, George. *The Chronology of the Life of Paul*, Epworth.

"Chronology of the New Testament," *New Bible Dictionary (Second Edition)*, InterVarsity Press.

Piper, John. "New Testament Chronology," *Encyclopedia of the Bible*, Baker.

Robinson, John A.T. *Redating the New Testament*, The Westminster Press.

Chronological and/or Dated Bibles

Acts in First-Person by the Men Who Lived It, SeedSowers.

Berkeley Version of the New Testament by Gerrit Verkuyl, Zondervan.

The Greatest Story by Johnston Cheney, Multnomah.

The Letters of Paul: An Expanded Paraphrase by F.F. Bruce, Eerdmans.

The Narrated Bible in Chronological Order by F. LaGard Smith, Harvest House.

The New Testament: A Translation by William Barclay, Westminster/John Knox Press.

The Seamless Bible, Destiny Image.

The Story of My Life as Told by Jesus Christ, SeedSowers.

Frank Viola's Series on Radical Church Reform

Volume 1: Rethinking the Wineskin: The Practice of the New Testament Church. This is Frank Viola's classic book on the first-century church. It compares and contrasts the practices of the early church with that of the modern institutional church.

Volume 2: Who is Your Covering? A Fresh Look at Leadership, Authority, and Accountability. This book explores the issues of church leadership and spiritual authority in much more depth than *Wineskin.*

Volume 3: Pagan Christianity: The Origins of Our Modern Church Practices. A unique work that traces every modern Protestant practice, proving that it has no root in the NT.

Volume 4: So You Want to Start a House Church? First-Century Styled Church Planting. A must read after completing *Rethinking the Wineskin.* This book discusses the apostolic pattern for planting NT-styled churches. It also answers the question: "What shall I do now that I have left the organized church?"

Volume 5: From Nazareth to Patmos: The Saga of the New Testament Church. Traces the growth and development of the Kingdom of God chronologically from Nazareth (the Gospels) to Patmos (Revelation).

Other Books by Frank Viola

Straight Talk to Elders. A hard-hitting message to pastors, elders, and ministers about God's idea of leadership.

Knowing Christ Together. An insightful book that explores the subject of knowing and walking with the Lord with other believers.

For these titles and more, visit **www.ptmin.org**
To correspond with the author, email him at **Violabooks@aol.com**

Additional copies of this book and other book titles from DESTINY IMAGE are available at your local bookstore.

For a complete list of our titles, visit us at www.destinyimage.com Send a request for a catalog to:

Destiny Image® Publishers, Inc.
P.O. Box 310
Shippensburg, PA 17257-0310

"Speaking to the Purposes of God for This Generation and for the Generations to Come"